Scaffolding With Storybooks

A Guide for Enhancing Young Children's Language and Literacy Achievement

Laura M. Justice
Khara L. Pence

With Angela R. Beckman,
Lori E. Skibbe,
and Alice K. Wiggins

University of Virginia
Charlottesville, Virginia, USA

INTERNATIONAL
Reading Association
800 BARKSDALE ROAD, PO BOX 8139
NEWARK, DE 19714-8139, USA
www.reading.org

The International Reading Association attempts, through its publications, to provide a forum for a wide spectrum of opinions on reading. This policy permits divergent viewpoints without implying the endorsement of the Association.

Director of Publications   Dan Mangan
Editorial Director, Books and Special Projects   Teresa Curto
Managing Editor, Books   Shannon T. Fortner
Acquisitions and Developmental Editor   Corinne M. Mooney
Associate Editor   Charlene M. Nichols
Associate Editor   Elizabeth C. Hunt
Production Editor   Amy Messick
Books and Inventory Assistant   Rebecca A. Zell
Permissions Editor   Janet S. Parrack
Assistant Permissions Editor   Tyanna L. Collins
Production Department Manager   Iona Muscella
Supervisor, Electronic Publishing   Anette Schütz
Senior Electronic Publishing Specialist   R. Lynn Harrison
Electronic Publishing Specialist   Lisa M. Kochel
Proofreader   Stacey Lynn Sharp

Project Editor   Elizabeth C. Hunt

Art   Cover Design, Linda Steere; Cover and Interior Illustrations, JupiterImages

Web addresses in this book were correct as of the publication date but may have become inactive or otherwise modified since that time. If you notice a deactivated or changed Web address, please e-mail books@reading.org with the words "Website Update" in the subject line. In your message, specify the Web link, the book title, and the page number on which the link appears.

Library of Congress Cataloging-in-Publication Data

Justice, Laura M., 1968-
  Scaffolding with storybooks : a guide for enhancing young children's language and literacy achievement / Laura M. Justice and Khara L. Pence with Angela R. Beckman ... [et al.].
    p. cm.
  Includes bibliographical references and index.
  ISBN 0-87207-578-8
  1. Language arts (Early childhood) 2. Reading (Early childhood) 3. Children--Books and reading. I. Pence, Khara L. II. Beckman, Angela. III. Title.
  LB1139.5.L35J87 2005
  372.6--dc22
                                                                                        2005016603

CONTENTS

PREFACE   vii

ACKNOWLEDGMENTS   xiv

CHAPTER 1   1

**Building Language and Literacy
Through Interactive Book Reading**

CHAPTER 2   13

**Building Print Knowledge:
Supporting Early Print Discoveries**

CHAPTER 3   26

**Building Word Knowledge:
Increasing the Complexity of Words
Children Understand and Produce**

CHAPTER 4   40

**Building Phonological Knowledge:
Developing a Sensitivity to Sound Units of Language**

CHAPTER 5   53

**Building Alphabet Knowledge:
Learning About the Features and Names of Letters**

CHAPTER 6   69

**Building Narrative Knowledge:
Extending Language to Share Experiences and Ideas**

CHAPTER 7   83

**Building World Knowledge:
Learning About the World Near and Far**

CONCLUSION   96

APPENDIX   97
Cross-Referencing List of All Storybooks

REFERENCES   111

CHILDREN'S LITERATURE CITED   117

INDEX   121

PREFACE

This book is an essential guide for those many individuals who serve as children's first teachers and who understand, as we do, that interactive book reading is an important context for helping children learn and develop. The activities and approaches we present are applicable to children from toddlerhood through first grade and also may be used to support the reading development of children who are in the early elementary grades and for whom reading is not arriving easily. The topics in this book are particularly relevant to professionals who work with children—reading specialists, literacy coaches, early interventionists, early childhood special educators, speech-language pathologists, school administrators, preschool teachers, primary educators, day-care providers, nannies, pediatricians, child psychologists, and social workers—and, of course, parents.

Rationale for This Book

We prepared this book to provide evidence-based suggestions for enhancing the language and literacy achievements of children from toddlerhood through the early elementary grades. We focus specifically on the context of shared storybook reading and how adults may capitalize on this interactive context to accelerate language and literacy learning for young children. Although we believe that all educators and the children with whom they work will benefit from the approaches described in this book, we believe these approaches will be particularly beneficial for children whose developmental trajectory is being steered off a healthy pathway due to environmental and developmental challenges such as poverty and disability. These children, more so than any others, are likely to struggle with reading across the elementary grades. As has been well documented in the research literature, once children start to struggle with reading, the odds are such that they will likely always struggle and that the gap between those who struggle and those who do not will widen gradually over time (Juel, 1988; K.E. Stanovich, 2000).

The prevalence of risk factors among U.S. schoolchildren affects many educators. Even those educators who work with toddlers and preschoolers see clear evidence of differences in the knowledge bases of those pupils who come from advantaged homes and those who do not. These educators must help these very young children enter kindergarten ready to learn and enabled to succeed in this increasingly academic context, which differs fundamentally from previous caregiving contexts at home and in the community. In turn, kindergarten educators must work

vii

to prepare all children to enter first grade, a significant challenge given that the majority of kindergarten teachers report that many of their students have serious problems transitioning to the academic milieu (Rimm-Kaufman, Pianta, & Cox, 2000). Indeed, the prevalence of risk factors among U.S. schoolchildren is astounding, and the impact of these risks on their achievements is significant. Large-scale national surveys show that almost half of U.S. kindergarten students experience at least one family risk factor upon their transition to school. Prevalent risk factors include being reared in poverty, residing in a single-parent household, having a parent with low educational attainment, and having a parent who speaks a language other than English (Rimm-Kaufman et al., 2000). As the number of risk factors experienced by a child increases, reading achievement decreases, with estimates from the U.S. Department of Education indicating that students' reading scores drop about 4 standard score points on standardized assessments of reading achievement for each familial risk factor present in a child's life (Rathbun & West, 2004). Within the current climate, which emphasizes not only accountability but also the arrival of "evidence-based progress to education" (P.J. Stanovich & Stanovich, 2003), preschool, kindergarten, and first-grade teachers are expected to meet students' literacy needs and equalize differences among students who enter school from remarkably diverse ethnic, linguistic, racial, and economic backgrounds. The political push for earlier and more intensive literacy interventions is driven in large part by national data showing that more than one third of U.S. fourth graders do not read proficiently (Johnson, 2004).

Our interest in preparing this book is to help all children build strong early foundations in language and literacy by providing educators with concrete approaches derived from the current research literature. These approaches not only will be beneficial to children whose language and literacy development is proceeding typically but also will make differences for those children who struggle due to environmental or developmental challenges. We capitalize upon the singularly important early childhood activity of adult–child storybook reading, which both research and practice show can be used to systematically build children's knowledge of language, literacy, and the world around them. The interactions between adults and children that occur within the storybook reading context take children from the here and now into a world that is metalinguistic, abstract, and imaginative. Through books, children learn words that are uncommonly experienced in their everyday lives, such as *sprouts*, *seahorses*, and *saucers*. Through books, children experience the abstraction of the alphabet letters and the sounds the letters represent repeatedly and under the guidance of a skilled adult. Through books, children are exposed to concepts that are abstract and difficult to talk about, such as emotions and thoughts. When engaged with storybooks in interactive routines by a sensitive adult, children develop the complex of readiness skills that will allow them to successfully navigate the academic rigors of learning to read in first grade and beyond.

Just reading books with children is certainly beneficial. However, research of the last decade has shown unequivocally that storybook reading interactions between children and adults can be manipulated to maximize children's gains from this important activity (e.g., Crain-Thoreson & Dale, 1999; Justice & Ezell, 2000; Wasik & Bond, 2001; Whitehurst et al., 1994). For instance, adults can point to print and track the print when they read to help develop children's interest in print and awareness of print forms and functions (Justice & Ezell, 2002). Likewise, adults can pause during reading sessions when they encounter unfamiliar words to define and talk about those words; this strategy builds children's vocabulary knowledge (Penno, Wilkinson, & Moore, 2002). Accumulating research literature shows that simply reading books with children is not as effective as embedding particular types of strategies or interactive behaviors into reading to systematically build children's skills in specific areas. While ensuring that all children are read to on a daily basis is an important goal for those who work with children and their families, the types of reading experiences in which children are engaged also must be of the highest quality and explicitly organized to promote those skills and concepts that children need to develop.

The ideas presented in this book are firmly grounded in our work as researchers in the Preschool Language and Literacy Lab at the University of Virginia. In our lab, we work with hundreds of young children each year as well as those individuals who are so important in their lives: preschool teachers, speech-language pathologists, literacy coaches, school administrators, and parents, among others. Our research focuses on identifying specific ways to advance children's early development, particularly in literacy and language. We are predominantly interested in strategies that respect the importance of children's social interactions with educators in their lives and that may have broad and long-lasting developmental consequences. We appreciate that there are subtle adjustments that adults can make when interacting with children that can have profound and positive consequences for children's development. For instance, by asking children fewer direct questions and by using more comments, adults can appreciably increase the amount of language children produce, which in turn helps build children's vocabulary and grammar skills. This book is grounded in this premise precisely, which is that adults can make minor adjustments when sharing books with children to have long-lasting positive developmental impacts.

The authors are a multidisciplinary team of individuals with backgrounds in developmental psychology, special education, early childhood education, reading education, speech-language pathology, computer science, and other fields. Laura Justice has been trained in education, English literature, and speech-language pathology and contributed expertise in evidence-based approaches to supporting early literacy development, particularly for at-risk learners. Khara Pence has been trained in education (cognition, development, and instruction) and contributed expertise in language acquisition and classroom processes that support children's language achievements. Angela Beckman has been trained in speech-language pathology and contributed expertise in language intervention for at-risk preschoolers and approaches to language facilitation. Lori Skibbe has been trained in developmental psychology and contributed expertise in parent–child interactions and scaffolding children's task performance. Alice Wiggins has been trained in computer science and elementary education and contributed expertise in supporting children's earliest accomplishments through dramatic play and other meaningful interactive experiences. We share a common interest in understanding early language and literacy development—including the problems children face that may prevent them from realizing their full potential. Thus, this book will be useful to many individuals as it infuses substantive knowledge and concepts from a variety of fields.

Organization of This Book

We have designed this book to be a practical resource for educators. Chapter 1 discusses major achievements in early language and literacy development and how interactive reading can support these achievements. After that introduction, each chapter focuses on one specific aspect of early childhood language and literacy that research shows can be facilitated through interactive reading: print knowledge, word knowledge, phonological knowledge, alphabet knowledge, narrative knowledge, and world knowledge. These six areas were selected because each has been linked empirically to early and later reading, social–behavioral, and more general academic achievement. By building early competencies and interests in these areas, educators who work with young children can play an important role in preparing children for later academic challenges and facilitating their transitions to more advanced levels of learning.

In each chapter, we present a list of objectives that are appropriate for children ranging in age from toddlerhood through early school age. These are not age-based objectives but rather are developmentally organized objectives that will pave the way to more advanced levels of learning. We demonstrate ways to approach these learning objectives through examples of adult–child storybook reading interactions in which adults and children work together to build children's knowledge and skills in the context of sensitive, developmentally appropriate scaffolding. *Scaffolding* is the term we use to describe the type and amount of assistance adults provide to children to support their learning. Adult scaffolding of children's learning is, in this book, delivered within the appealing and comfortable context of the storybook reading interaction. We believe that this context, because it is comfortable and familiar to children—becoming more so over time—provides a supportive framework in which adults can teach and children can learn.

In chapter 2, Angela Beckman presents approaches and ideas for helping children develop print knowledge. Print knowledge is an important aspect of preschool and kindergarten literacy development, and it describes children's knowledge about and interest in the orthography of their written language. During the first six years of life, children begin to view written language as an object worthy of their attention and gradually come to understand how written language is organized, the names of various print units (e.g., letters, words), and the way in which print is used to convey meaning. Children acquire much of this information incidentally as they interact with print in their homes and communities. Interactions with storybooks are a particularly useful venue for adults to reveal the mysteries and idiosyncrasies of print to young children.

In chapter 3, we discuss ways to develop children's word knowledge, or vocabulary. A child's vocabulary knowledge during the first six years of life is predictive of later reading comprehension abilities; thus, we want to maximize children's achievements in vocabulary during their first six years and give them the tools for precisely representing their world and thoughts through words. As most adults who interact regularly with children know, young children are quite skilled at learning new words with even one exposure to the word. The pace of early vocabulary development sets the stage for the child's ongoing language and literacy learning over the academic years (Beck, McKeown, & Kucan, 2002). Children who have a large vocabulary are better able to acquire new words during reading and formal instruction, possibly because they do not have to devote resources to learning those words that they already know or understand (Robbins & Ehri, 1994; Senechal, Thomas, & Monker, 1995). Therefore, early childhood is a time in which children require many experiences with words, and books provide children a ready and accessible world of words that infrequently occur in their homes and classrooms.

In chapter 4, Lori Skibbe presents approaches to using storybooks to foster children's phonological knowledge, specifically their phonological awareness. Phonological awareness describes children's sensitivities to the sound structure of oral language. Preschool and kindergarten are a critically important time for helping children develop these sensitivities and for ensuring that children arrive at formal reading instruction in first grade with a well-developed awareness of phonological segments. Major achievements prior to first grade include, for instance, being sensitive to rhyme and alliteration. Researchers have shown that children who have phonological awareness are better able to profit from reading instruction, as this requires a threshold of phonological sensitivity. Children who begin reading instruction with well-developed phonological awareness learn more quickly and easily compared to children who do not have these sensitivities (Anthony, Lonigan, Driscoll, Phillips, & Burgess, 2003; Storch & Whitehurst, 2002).

In chapter 5, we describe objectives and approaches to supporting children's alphabet knowledge. Alphabet knowledge is, by some accounts, the single best predictor of elementary-grade achievement in word recognition (Adams, 1990). During the preschool years, educators should help children to develop fluent, skilled recognition of the alphabet letters so that later reading instruction can build on this achievement. Learning about the alphabet need not be a tedious chore of early childhood. If adults show children that they view the alphabet as an object of interest that warrants their attention, children will likely develop a similar affinity. Storybook reading interactions between children and adults are an exemplary context for discussions about the alphabet: how it works, why it is important, and what the various symbols stand for.

In chapter 6, we discuss approaches to supporting children's early achievements in narrative knowledge. Narrative is a multidimensional language skill that has its roots in early childhood. Narrative is a type of discourse in which an individual shares a real or fictional event through spoken or written language. In childhood, adolescence, and adulthood, much of our conversation features narrative as we relay personal experiences, give instructions, reason about future activities, and the like. Narrative is a particularly demanding language skill because it requires the speaker to integrate careful attention to syntax, vocabulary and word selection, and the needs of the speaker. We selected narrative as a key language goal because narrative competence draws together children's linguistic resources across syntax, vocabulary, and pragmatics, and it is academically and socially relevant. By helping children develop narrative skills, educators are in fact helping children develop a large set of linguistic skills.

In the final chapter, chapter 7, Alice Wiggins describes approaches to supporting children's world knowledge. World knowledge intersects a variety of important developmental domains, including literacy, language, and cognition. Children's early experiences provide them with a map of the world and give them labels to represent this world. Storybooks are a critical source for furthering children's early world knowledge because they provide children with access to a world that exists beyond the here and now. They introduce children to ideas, concepts, people, and places that may not be available to them in their homes, communities, and schools. This final chapter provides specific resources to guide early educators in opening up a world of knowledge to children through storybooks.

The appendix contains a table listing of all the storybooks we have used in the chapter activities and provides suggestions for the kinds of concepts we believe each storybook best illustrates. Adults can use the appendix to plan reading sessions with children that use the same storybook to address multiple concepts.

This book provides a practical resource for those many professionals who work with young children from toddlerhood into the early elementary grades. We have drawn from the current research evidence on approaches that support language and literacy achievements in young children to provide a readily usable and practical guide for professionals that can directly inform practices in classrooms, clinics, and homes. The techniques, strategies, and activities presented throughout this book are derived from the basic premise that making simple adjustments to the way we read with children can result in positive and potentially long-lasting influences on children's language and literacy skills. Chapter 1 provides a more in-depth description of interactive book reading and children's key accomplishments in language and literacy from toddlerhood into the early elementary grades.

ACKNOWLEDGMENTS

This book is an integration of ideas from our ongoing work in the field and in the lab. Our understanding of child development and the use of storybooks to enhance specific achievements is continually fostered through conversations with teachers, parents, children, administrators, policymakers, and researchers. We would particularly like to thank the teachers, families, and administrators who have collaborated with us at Wise County Public Schools, Culpeper Head Start, Culpeper County Public Schools, Webster County Public Schools, Charlottesville City Schools, Greene County Child Care Center, Wesley Community Child Care Center, and the Phonological Awareness and Literacy Screening Project at the University of Virginia.

We have many fine colleagues at the University of Virginia who support our work and provide us with a collegial and enlightening atmosphere in which to share our ideas and to think through perplexing concepts. Requiring special mention are Robert Pianta, Sara Rimm-Kaufman, Marcia Invernizzi, Dan Hallahan, Laura Smolkin, Allison Hall, Marianne Lampert, and Ryan Bowles. Helen Ezell at the University of Pittsburgh, Joan Kaderavek at the University of Toledo, Teresa Ukrainetz at the University of Wyoming, and Melanie Schuele at Vanderbilt University also serve regularly as sounding boards for our ideas, thoughts, and plans, and for this we are thankful.

CHAPTER 1

Building Language and Literacy Through Interactive Book Reading

Interactive book reading describes shared book reading interactions between adults and children that go beyond the traditional routine in which the adult reads the text while the child listens. During interactive reading, both the child and adult are active participants in the construction of a dialogue surrounding the storybook. This dialogue might focus on the story line, such as characters, events, or settings; experiences the child has had that are similar to those contained in the book; or specific words, aspects of print, or concepts that are novel to the child. A key feature of interactive reading is the *intentionality* of the adult reader, who carefully structures the interactive reading experience to purposefully "challenge, extend, and scaffold children's skills" to propel children forward on their path of learning (Pianta & La Paro, 2003, p. 28). Drawing upon developmental concepts first articulated by the Soviet psychologist Lev Vygotsky (1930/1978, 1934/1986), the intentional adult utilizes the interactive reading experience to create dialogues with children that capitalize upon what children already know to veer them toward what they do not yet know.

Some skilled adults regularly use an interactive reading approach when reading with children in the classroom or at home. However, not all children experience interactive reading of sufficient quality and quantity. In fact, both the quality and quantity of children's book reading experiences vary immensely, according to studies that have looked closely at reading interactions in children's homes and in their classrooms (e.g., Dickinson & Keebler, 1989; Hammett, van Kleeck, & Huberty, 2003; McGill-Franzen, Lanford, & Adams, 2002; Sonnenschein & Munsterman, 2002; Yaden, Smolkin, & Conlon, 1989). Studies of how educators share books with children show great variability in the extent to which interaction is a salient feature (e.g., McGill-Franzen et al., 2002), and studies of parents reading with their children at home show the predominant approach to be one of limited interaction (Hammett et al., 2003). Some research shows that the way adults share books with children is culturally influenced (van Kleeck, Stahl, & Bauer, 2003), which makes sense given that the way individuals interact with one another in general is greatly influenced by cultural values, beliefs, and preferences. With this in mind, we argue the importance of providing *all* children with frequent and high-quality interactive reading opportunities but also respect the individual preferences and approaches of educators and parents, recognizing that various approaches may have complementary benefits to children. Children can experience interactive reading in addition to other types of reading experiences, which together may build their developing competencies in complementary ways.

Interactive Book Reading, Risk, and Resilience

By naming Public Law 107-110 the No Child Left Behind Act of 2001 (NCLB, 2002) policymakers explicitly noted that disproportionate numbers of children are indeed being left behind in U.S. schools, notably in the area of reading specifically and literacy more generally. This condition is mainly true for children who are poor, who are of minority ethnic or racial backgrounds, who speak English as a second language, or who have disabilities (Johnson, 2004), although nearly one fifth of children with no evident disadvantages also face challenges in achieving literacy. As an example, consider that 43% of U.S. fourth graders qualifying for free or reduced lunch do not read proficiently, compared to 18% of those students who do not qualify for this program. Consider also that 46% of African American fourth graders and 44% of Hispanic fourth graders do not achieve even a basic level of reading competence (Johnson, 2004). Clearly, statistics such as these point out a problem of epidemic proportions that affects the economic and social prosperity of the United States. As educators, we recognize that solutions to reading challenges must begin early in a child's life before difficulties are permitted to emerge. Once a reading delay manifests for a particular child in elementary school, the odds suggest that a return to healthy progress is unlikely (Francis, Shaywitz, Stuebing, Shaywitz, & Fletcher, 1996). Accordingly, experts advocate the need to "catch children *before* they fall" by allocating resources toward prevention of reading problems (Torgesen, 1998).

It is our contention (and that of many others) that the academic and social risks experienced by economically disadvantaged students in the area of reading begin well prior to entering elementary school and that preventive interventions must be directed early in children's lives to promote resilience and reduce risk for academic problems in the elementary grades. One of the better documented risk factors for later academic difficulties relates to early language and literacy development: Children reared in poverty exhibit underdeveloped skills in print knowledge, word knowledge and vocabulary, phonological awareness, alphabet knowledge, and narrative skills compared to children reared in more advantaged circumstances (e.g., Bowey, 1995; Chaney, 1994; Hoff-Ginsberg, 1998; Justice & Ezell, 2001; Lonigan et al., 1999). Underdeveloped skills in language and literacy during early childhood may contribute to later difficulties with higher level application of these skills to academic language and literacy tasks, such as word decoding and reading comprehension, and also have been linked to short- and long-term problems with social–relational skills (e.g., Catts, Fey, Tomblin, & Zhang, 2002; Fujiki, Brinton, & Clarke, 2002). At the same time, these early disadvantages impede children's successful adjustment to the academic rigors of the kindergarten and first-grade learning environments, which are often qualitatively different than previous caregiving milieus and which present a unique set of challenges to at-risk children (Rimm-Kaufman, Pianta, & Cox, 2000).

As educators and policymakers consider proactive approaches to increasing the academic success of at-risk students, there is consensus (see Snow, Burns, & Griffin, 1998) across these constituencies that evidence-based educational interventions must utilize preemptive moves through *primary prevention*. Contrasted with *secondary prevention* (interventions to slow or reverse the course of reading problems once they emerge in first grade and beyond) and *tertiary prevention* (interventions to support one's ability to compensate for a reading problem that is serious and persistent), primary prevention focuses on preventing reading difficulties from emerging in the first place, thereby reducing the need for more intensive, expensive, and time-consuming secondary and tertiary preventions (Kauffman, 1999). Presumably, an effective primary prevention will ease children's transition to the rigors of academic instruction in kindergarten and first grade and provide the first in a series of accumulating successes in achieving literacy. In short, primary preventions will ensure children's readiness to succeed as they move through the increasingly challenging rigors of academic instruction.

Readiness for reading instruction is a complex notion, as there are many elements of development that enable (or disable) young children to successfully profit from beginning reading instruction. Although much attention has been directed in recent years to phonological awareness as a particularly crucial reading-readiness skill, other aspects of children's development are just as important for enabling their early success as readers. These include, for instance, children's vocabulary repertoire, or word knowledge, and their knowledge of people, places, and events in our world, or world knowledge. Early educators, including teachers and parents, must help children develop a solid foundation for language, literacy, and knowledge of the world around them.

The readiness concept underscores the importance of promoting children's early learning foundations so that they are able to engage immediately with formal academic learning that characterizes first grade and beyond. While the concept of school readiness often is taken as an emphasis on children's skills and what they know, this concept also emphasizes the "goodness of fit" between children and the contexts in which they learn, and the importance of their sustained engagement in high-quality interactions with their primary caregivers, including parents and teachers. Our colleague Robert Pianta at the University of Virginia has written that children's readiness emerges after a period of several years when children have engaged in sensitive, nurturing, and enjoyable interactions with stable and consistent adults (Pianta & La Paro, 2003). Through these interactions, children experience regular routines and rhythms and engage with materials that stimulate and challenge them to develop mastery of various concepts. This concept of readiness, which emphasizes not only children's skill development but also the *contexts* and *interactions* within which children develop these skills, lays the foundation for this book. In this book, we emphasize adult–child interactive storybook reading as a critical context through which sensitive and nurturing conversations pave the way for the child's achievement of numerous important concepts about language and literacy. In the next sections, we focus our discussion on summarizing children's preschool and kindergarten achievements in language and literacy, describing the role of interactive reading in promoting children's language and literacy, and discussing essential characteristics of effective interactive reading.

Preschool and Kindergarten Achievements in Language and Literacy

Language and *literacy* are separate constructs that develop in distinct yet overlapping and reciprocal ways. In the period of development from birth through about 6 years of age, children's language and literacy accomplishments are numerous. This period contains, in fact, a greater series of developmental achievement in these areas than any time to come in the child's future. The next sections provide a general overview of language accomplishments during the first six years of life; for further detail, see Berko Gleason (2005), Hoff (2001), and Owens (2005).

    Language is characteristically defined as the rule-governed symbol system used to represent thoughts and ideas. Language is a tool used for spoken, signed, or written communication, and it comprises five domains. (1) *Phonology* is the set of rules governing the sound system of language, or the specific sounds used by a given language to generate syllables and words. Standard American English uses approximately 40 phonemes, or speech sounds, plus or minus a few depending on the particular dialect. (2) *Syntax* is the set of rules governing the organization of sentences, or the way in which underlying propositions are organized at a structural level (for instance, the linear organization of *the + brown + bear* to fill the object slot in a sentence). (3) *Morphology* is the set of rules governing the structure of words, such as how suffixes can be added to words for inflection (e.g., plural, possessive) and how prefixes and suffixes can be added to words to change meaning (e.g., *sleep* versus *sleepless*; *preview* versus *view*). (4) *Semantics* is the set of rules governing the meaning of words and sentences and includes the receptive and expressive vocabulary of an individual and one's ability to efficiently access this vocabulary to precisely and effectively communicate.

(5) *Pragmatics* is the set of rules governing the effective use of language for communicative and social purposes; these rules include, for instance, knowing how much information to provide a listener, knowing how to organize a story cohesively, and understanding how to take turns and when to interject.

In the years following birth, children rapidly acquire the rules governing each of these five domains. In phonology, children develop underlying representations of all the phonemes of their language by the end of their first year of life and are able to produce these sounds with precision by about 7 years of age. In syntax, children develop an adult-like syntactic system by about 5 years of age. By this time, children's sentence structure is fully developed such that children can produce complex and compound sentences with full subjects and predicates. In morphology, children have a comprehensive set of inflections by 5 years of age that they can use to inflect words, including the present-progressive marker (*-ing*), the plural and possessive markers (*-s*, *-'s*), past-tense verb markers (*-ed*), and contracted copula and auxiliary verbs (you*'re*, I*'m*). Children by 5 years of age readily use prefixes and suffixes to manipulate words and to further develop their vocabulary repertoire. In semantics, children have a receptive vocabulary of several thousand words by 5 years of age and can readily arrange words into conceptual categories, such as colors, places, and emotions. In pragmatics, children can engage in extended discourse of four or more turns by the end of preschool and understand how to use language to serve a variety of purposes: to reason, to explain, to negate, to hypothesize, to reject, and to comment. For all intents and purposes, by the time children enter first grade, their language system—including all five of its rule-governed domains—is fully formed and adult-like. Children continue to *refine* their linguistic capabilities in the years to come, although the system is in place and unlikely to develop at the same pace or in the same way as it did during the previous six years.

Simultaneous to these remarkable achievements in language, children are beginning to make sense of the world of literacy, to include reading and writing. *Literacy* is used in this book to describe an individual's ability to use language as a written tool for reading and writing, and a key aspect of literacy is being able to read. In this book, we define *reading* (*R*) as the multiplicative product of decoding (*D*) and language comprehension (*C*), or $D \times C = R$ (Gough & Tunmer, 1986), to emphasize the necessary role of both decoding and comprehension in children's success at reading. Seminal models of reading development (e.g., Chall, 1983; Ehri, 1991) describe children's progress as readers as a series of important transitions from emergent literacy (prealphabetic), to beginning reading (decoding), to conventional reading (reading for meaning). Instruction that follows such models emphasizes the child's development of prealphabetic competencies, followed by decoding ability, to arrive at the ability to read for meaning, or comprehend. The child's earliest developments in reading thus involve acquiring decoding prerequisites at the same time as the child is progressing in the oral language achievements discussed in previous sections (phonology, syntax, morphology, semantics, and pragmatics).

The alphabetic code is a rule-governed system in which letters of the alphabet represent the spoken sounds or combinations of sounds of language. For instance, the letter *K* represents the /k/ sound, whereas the letter *S* represents the /s/ sound, and the letter *X* (as in *tax*) represents the combination of the /k/ and /s/ sounds. Writing and reading both require that an individual unlock the alphabetic code, or represent the systematic relationships between letters and sounds. Although the way in which children have been taught to unlock the alphabetic code—as well as the extent to which this should be emphasized in early reading instruction—has long been a source of considerable controversy, most scholars recognize that children's early reading success is dependent upon their ability to understand and represent the relationships between letters and sounds (e.g., National Institute of Child Health and Human Development [NICHD], 2000a; Storch & Whitehurst, 2002; Stuart, 1995).

For children to make sense of the relationships between letters and sounds—which is likely to be an important part of reading instruction in first and second grades—they must arrive at that instruction with a well-developed sense of print and of sound. These two areas of early literacy development are referred to, respectively, as *written language awareness* and *phonological awareness*, and they represent two critical dimensions of preschool and kindergarten literacy development.

Written language awareness describes children's knowledge about how print works: what it is used for and how it is organized. In the years spanning from birth through kindergarten, children reared in print-rich homes and communities realize that print is an object worthy of their attention, that print carries important information, that print is arranged in unique and systematic ways, and that print forms have specific names (Chaney, 1998; Justice & Ezell, 2001; Lonigan, Burgess, Anthony, & Barker, 1998). We have described these major achievements as comprising *print interest*, *print functions*, *print conventions*, *print forms*, and *print part-to-whole relationships* (Justice & Ezell, 2004). *Print interest* refers to children's coming to view print as an object warranting attention as a distinct type of environmental stimulus. We view the achievement of print interest as an early watershed event in emergent literacy, on the basis that this provides a vehicle through which children will, on their own, readily and rapidly accumulate familiarity with print forms and functions. *Print functions* refer to children's awareness that print provides meaning to events and additional detail beyond other stimuli (e.g., pictures). *Print conventions* describe children's growing knowledge of the idiosyncratic ways in which print is organized for various genres. *Print forms* describe children's understanding that words, letters, and other print units have distinct names and are used in specific, organized ways. *Print part-to-whole relationships* describe children's growing knowledge of the combinatorial properties of print units, such as how letters make up words and that words can be linked to create larger propositions. The most parsimonious model for organizing children's achievements in written language awareness is to differentiate between *print knowledge*, or the idiosyncrasies of print organization across different discourse units and texts, and *alphabet knowledge*, or the names and distinctive features of the 26 alphabet letters. By the end of kindergarten, children with sophisticated knowledge in these areas are well prepared to make sense of how print and sound work together in the alphabetic system.

Phonological awareness describes children's knowledge about the sound structure of language, specifically that language is organized phonologically. Phonological awareness refers to a child's ability to focus explicitly or implicitly on the sound characteristics of a word or syllable, for instance, that two words share initial consonants (e.g., *b*ig, *b*ill), that a word has four syllables (e.g., *al-li-ga-tor*), that two words share a rime unit (e.g., h*at*, m*at*), or that a word has three sounds (e.g., /p/ /I/ /t/). Children gradually develop their sensitivity to the phonological structure of language from birth through the end of first grade. Early accomplishments in phonological awareness include recognizing that sentences are made up of words, that words are made up of syllables, and that two words can rhyme. In the later preschool years, children recognize when two words share sounds in the beginning or final position of words, and typically in the kindergarten year they are able to blend sounds to make words and segment words into their constituent sounds. In first grade, children typically become able to focus more intensely on the phonemic structure of words and syllables and to think about phonemes as distinct features of language. With this knowledge, children are better able to decipher the alphabetic system of written English and to profit from instruction that requires more advanced levels of phonological awareness.

The Role of Interactive Reading in Promoting Language and Literacy

Young children acquire a significant portion of their language and literacy knowledge and skills through informal and naturalistic interactions with the adults in their lives. In comparison, relatively little language and literacy are developed through direct, didactic instruction. Children are biologically and socially geared toward feasting on the knowledge and concepts they experience when interacting with others, and through this incidental feasting, children rapidly and apparently effortlessly develop an abundance of knowledge about oral and written language.

Adult–child interactive storybook reading, in particular, is viewed by many experts as one of the most potent and frequent contexts for this incidental language and literacy learning of young children (e.g., Bus, 2001; Teale, 1986; Whitehurst & Lonigan, 1998). Shared book reading is seen as particularly powerful because it is a context that is meaningful, interesting, and motivating to young children. Hypothetically, children's language and literacy are advanced within such interactions as a function of both adult and child contributions; the adult deliberately encourages and scaffolds the child's engagement and participation while the child extracts meaning and constructs knowledge. The adult's involvement is sensitive to the changing needs and contributions of the child, whereas the child's needs and contributions reflect the adult's dynamic sensitivities. Repeated engagement in these bidirectional and dynamic interchanges results in the successful transmission of language and literacy knowledge from adult to child.

The activities and approaches used in this book to further children's early development in language and literacy are based on this theoretical perspective, that is, in the value of early interactive reading for skill development and that the social interaction between adult and child can be modulated to more effectively promote children's learning. Of particular importance to our perspective of early learning is the role of *scaffolding by the intentional adult* to assist children's progressive movement from dependent to independent performance in a particular skill or area of knowledge.

Scaffolding is a metaphoric term that describes the assistance provided by an adult to a child that moves the child to increasingly independent and higher levels of performance. An adult question during interactive reading—such as "Why is the boy running?"—may be a scaffold for one child but not for another. Conversing about the abstract notion of "why" is far beyond the grasp of a child who is just developing language skills and speaks in one-word utterances. On the other hand, for a child with slightly more developed language skills, a conversation focused on why the boy is running may stimulate and support linguistic and cognitive developments. Scaffolding is used in tasks that are whole and complete, not broken down into their smaller task components. For instance, an adult can support a child to consider the meaning of the word *blooming* as it occurs in the context of a fictional storybook. Scaffolding is distinct from *shaping*, which is another type of instructional approach used to promote children's learning. With *shaping*, a particular aspect of skill or knowledge is broken down into its smallest components; the adult teaches the child each component of the task until the child achieves mastery. Eventually, the child reaches the whole, complex task and can perform it successfully because all of its smaller components have been learned and mastered. An adult using shaping might first teach a child the word *blooming* in a highly structured task in which the stimulus is just the word itself rather than the word embedded in discourse (e.g., in a fictional storybook). Once the child has come to understand the word *blooming* at this level—as a single word removed from context—the adult can help the child to understand it in phrases, sentences, and discourse. By contrast, with scaffolding the adult grounds instruction in whole, complex tasks and manipulates the support provided to the child to intentionally advance the child's learning.

Scaffolding and shaping can be combined to maximize learning and teaching. An adult can identify specific components of a larger task that a child should learn, or at least be exposed to, and help the child apply these components within a larger complex task. For instance, an adult might help a child learn about alphabet letters within a storybook reading session, which shows the application of the knowledge to the larger act of reading.

Not all adult behaviors or input are scaffolds. For a particular behavior or type of input to be considered a scaffold, it must enable children to work at a higher level of performance than they would be able to do on their own (Bruner, 1978; Vygotsky, 1930/1978, 1934/1986). Scaffolding is most effective when it helps children perform at a level that is much higher than what they can do alone, rather than moving children incrementally along the path of learning and development. This is an important concept, so we will restate it: *The adult uses scaffolding to help children perform at a level that is much higher than the children can achieve on their own.* What this means is that adults need to be sensitive to what an individual child cannot do and then enable the child to do it—which, to some, might seem to be developmentally inappropriate. For instance, if an adult asks a child to write her name, the child might rightfully say, "But I can't write!" The adult uses scaffolding, though, to engage the child at a level that is beyond her own capabilities. Here, the adult can introduce a variety of possible scaffolds to promote learning, such as writing the child's name so she can trace or copy it, dictating letters so the child can write them, or cupping the child's hand in her own to make the letters. Scaffolding is developmentally appropriate if the child is not frustrated and if the adult provides the support needed for the child to be successful.

Types of adult behaviors and input that seem particularly useful in engaging children at high levels of performance and fostering children's rapid movement from dependent to independent levels of performance include the following:

- *Distancing scaffolds*: Distancing scaffolds are used by the adult to gradually reduce the amount of support given to the child, to relinquish control of the activity, and to transfer the performance from the social realm to the child's inner psychological realm. Distancing scaffolds include commenting on the child's competence (e.g., "You are doing this so well!") and past performance (e.g., "Remember, you have done this before."), as well as decreasing physical assistance (e.g., pointing) (Diaz, Neal, & Vachio, 1990; Lidz & Pena, 1996; Ukrainetz, 1998).

- *Linguistic scaffolds*: Linguistic scaffolds are used by the adult to present advanced models of language and literacy that build directly on the child's level of knowledge or skill. Linguistic scaffolds include asking open-ended questions (e.g., "What is going to happen next?"), describing unfamiliar concepts or ideas (e.g., "He feels *frustrated*. See the look on his face? Sort of sad, sort of angry. That is *frustrated*."), and recasting and expanding the child's own verbalizations (Child: "It's a letter *B*." Adult: "Right. It's an uppercase letter *B*.") (Girolametto, Pearce, & Weitzman, 1996; Justice & Ezell, 2000).

- *Regulatory scaffolds*: Adults use regulatory scaffolds to help children understand a specific task or goal and how it applies to a larger goal. These include, for instance, describing how small tasks or skills apply to a larger whole (e.g., "Knowing these letters will help you read these words."), discussing task components (e.g., "To read this word, you need to look at each letter."), and helping a child to evaluate his own performance (e.g., "How did you think you did?") (Diaz et al., 1990; Feuerstein, 1980; Greenfield, 1984).

- *Structural scaffolds*: Structural scaffolds are specific aspects of the context in which learning takes place that help to improve or support children's learning. For instance, an activity might be motivating and appealing to a child, which helps to engage the child and thus serves as a type of scaffold. Structural scaffolds include, for example, working in a known and familiar routine and working with motivating and appealing materials. Involving peers in an activity is also a type of structural scaffold, if the peers model advanced language or literacy forms or functions. By using storybooks as a tool to foster children's language and literacy, as emphasized throughout this book, the adult makes use of an important structural scaffold: the adult–child shared storybook reading routine. For many children, books provide a familiar and known routine. They understand how books work and how interactions over books should occur. Reading books repeatedly with children serves as a structural scaffold because it breeds familiarity. For children who do not have this familiarity with books, it is useful to build this knowledge base so that this structural scaffold can support learning. Additionally, books themselves, by being appealing and engaging to the child, provide another structural scaffold. The storybooks used as examples in this book were selected for their special appeal to children and the likelihood that they can provide an extra scaffold to support children's learning (Ukrainetz, 1998).

Essential Characteristics of Effective Interactive Reading

In this book, we present a variety of read-aloud strategies along with the titles of excellent storybooks for building children's knowledge and skills in different areas. We provide transcripts of adults and children in interactive routines, but we do not mean these to be scripts that should be followed. We view interactive reading as a context that is fluid, dynamic, and bidirectional as the adult and child respond to each other's contributions. The transcripts we provide are used to illustrate what high-quality reading interactions between adults and children might look like, and how adults can scaffold different targets of learning. However, certain qualities of effective interactive reading cannot be captured in any transcript. Keep in mind the following essential characteristics of high-quality reading interactions:

- *Adult sensitivity and responsiveness*: The most important characteristic of adults who are reading books with children (or engaging in any activity with children for that matter) is that they be sensitive and responsive partners. Adults who are sensitive and responsive show children that they value the children's contributions to the storybook reading interaction (Bus & Van IJzendoorn, 1995; Leseman & de Jong, 1998). Weitzman and Greenberg (2002) offer strategies for engaging with children in a responsive manner, which include *observing*, *waiting*, *listening*, and *being face-to-face*. Adults who *observe* not only are on the lookout for verbal responses and initiations but also watch for children's facial expressions, body posture, and eye gaze, which can indicate how engaged and motivated they are and how well they understand new concepts. Adults who *wait* give children plenty of time to formulate their responses and reply. The adult leans forward and looks expectantly while pausing to signal to the child an interest in her contributions. The adult who waits also recognizes that young children need more time than adults to formulate responses to questions and comments. Weitzman and Greenberg (2002) suggest that adults count to 10 to allow the child ample time to respond. Adults who *listen* pay close attention to what the child is saying so as to respond appropriately to keep the conversation going. During the storybook reading interaction, it is also important to *sit face-to-face* at the physical level of the child. Weitzman and Greenberg (2002) suggest that being face-to-face with a child brings a special physical and emotional connection to the interaction and may be particularly helpful for those children who are generally reluctant to respond or who have their own agenda before the storybook interaction begins.

- *Child engagement*: An additional and critical quality of the effective interactive reading exchange is the engaged child (Schneider & Hecht, 1995). Engagement and persistence on the part of children are to some extent related to temperament; however, adults can foster those qualities in children by manipulating the context. We encourage adults to ensure child engagement in all reading sessions, which may be enhanced by allowing the child to label pictures and ask and answer questions during storybook reading. Having children answer questions during storybook readings can help to produce greater gains in their expressive vocabulary than reading passively, although passive exposure to novel concepts is an important feature of the shared reading experience (Senechal, 1997). Moreover, children may get greater enjoyment out of storybook reading when they actively contribute to the interaction. Allow children to set the pace of reading interactions—pausing to look at pictures, talking about words, and exploring topics of particular interest. Allow children to handle reading materials and to turn pages. Remember that deviations from the text can be beneficial. The object of book reading sessions should not be to get through the book or only to read the words on the page but rather to create an enjoyable, high-quality, and sensitive interaction.

• *Repeated reading*: Children enjoy reading books multiple times, through which they gain ownership of the experience and familiarity with the text that, in turn, enables them to make new discoveries. Single readings of storybooks have been found to be insufficient for children's retention of new vocabulary, whereas multiple readings of storybooks have been found to facilitate the acquisition of both expressive vocabulary (the words children produce) and receptive vocabulary (the words children understand) (e.g., Justice, 2002; Penno, Wilkinson, & Moore, 2002; Robbins & Ehri, 1994). Repeated readings also create a sense of familiarity for children, and through the reinforcement of known concepts, children will become more and more confident in their prereading skills. Learning within a familiar context and with familiar materials provides a structural scaffold that fosters children's learning of new concepts and skills (Wasik & Bond, 2001).

Interactive storybook reading between adults and young children is an important context for developing children's skills and knowledge in many areas. This chapter provided an overview of children's many accomplishments in language and literacy that occur from birth through the early-elementary grades. We discussed how interactive storybook reading experiences can provide children with explicit yet meaningful opportunities to develop and refine their skills in numerous aspects of language and literacy. Although later chapters present specific strategies and approaches to target different areas of development, such as print knowledge or phonological awareness, we emphasize the importance of embedding targeted instruction within an interactive routine in which the adult is a sensitive and responsive partner.

In the next chapter, we focus on an area of child development that can be explicitly yet sensitively targeted through interactive reading. Chapter 2 describes young children's development of print knowledge and explores ways in which adult–child interactive reading can be modified to enhance children's skills, knowledge, and interests related to print.

Building Print Knowledge: Supporting Early Print Discoveries

P rint knowledge is a key dimension of emergent and early literacy development. *Print knowledge* encompasses children's knowledge about printed letters, words, and book conventions. Some specific aspects of print knowledge include understanding the distinction between print and pictures, understanding that print carries meaning, and understanding how to hold a book, turn pages in a book, and read from left to right (Justice & Ezell, 2004). Print knowledge contributes to literacy development by providing children an essential tool for translating the alphabetic code to decode words; in turn, children who are able to fluently decode are able to focus their cognitive resources on making sense of what they read.

How Print Knowledge Develops

Adults may notice that children who have not yet begun to read tend to focus on the pictures rather than print during storybook reading interactions. When preschool children share books with adults, about 95% of their visual attention is directed at the illustrations in the storybook (Justice & Lankford, 2002) and 95% of children's talk during shared reading focuses on illustrations or concepts expressed in the storybook (Ezell & Justice, 2000; Phillips & McNaughton, 1990; Yaden et al., 1989). With the help of an adult, children can be guided to explore the print within storybooks as an object worthy of their attention (Justice & Ezell, 2004).

Print knowledge is an important aspect of emergent literacy that develops gradually over the course of early childhood; evidence of print knowledge development may emerge in the toddler years (Goodman, 1986; van Kleeck, 1998). Young children demonstrate print knowledge in several ways. First, children demonstrate an increased attention to and awareness of print in their environment. They may begin to point out familiar letters ("That letter is in my name."), recognize words that they see frequently (e.g., the word *STOP* on a stop sign), or inquire about letters and words that are unfamiliar ("What does that word say?"). Second, children develop an understanding of the functions that different forms of print can convey. For example, they understand the difference between print that they see on road signs and print that they see in newspapers and on menus. Third, children develop an understanding of the set of idiosyncratic conventions that govern print presentations, including left-to-right directionality and spacing between words. Children with this understanding are able to identify where to begin reading on a page, which direction to read a page, and how to turn the pages in a book. Fourth, children begin to develop the ability to associate words spoken aloud with words in print. This means that if adults read a simple sentence aloud to children while looking at a book, the children will be able to point to some or all of the words, in the correct order, as each word is read slowly. Finally, children recognize the way in which print units are organized for written language purposes, such as how letters are grouped to form words and words are grouped to make phrases and sentences (Hiebert, 1981; Justice & Ezell, 2004; Lomax & McGee, 1987).

Within the context of shared storybook reading, one of the first signs that children are attending to the organization and functions of print is memorization of lines of text and pretend reading of stories (Adams, 1990; Snow et al., 1998). Adults can capitalize on this print interest and create a literacy-rich environment in the following ways: (1) demonstrate the value literacy holds by modeling reading and encouraging children to read; (2) respond to children's interest in reading and set expectations for them to participate in reading; (3) ensure that appropriate reading materials are available and accessible to children; and (4) read with children and encourage verbal interactions that extend beyond the text on the page (Adams, 1990; Snow et al., 1998). To help children in all of these areas, particularly the fourth point, which emphasizes children's participation in verbal interactions that go beyond the text on the page, it is important that adults reference print within storybooks to show children that print is interesting and worthy of discussion. Through these conversations, adults can guide children to understand how print is organized, its various functions, and its relationship to the more global act of reading for meaning. Helping parents to support their children's print knowledge in the home environment is an important goal of early education. On the next page, we provide some tips for parents to guide your efforts.

How Interactive Reading Supports the Development of Print Knowledge

Interactive reading offers a natural and authentic context through which adults can help children establish the relationship between spoken and written language and learn more about how print works. As adults and children engage in interactive reading, adults can make references to print in simple and unobtrusive ways. Ezell and

print Knowledge
Tips for parents

Parents can foster their children's print knowledge throughout the day using a variety of authentic experiences. It is important for parents to guide children's interaction with print placed throughout the home environment; just placing print around the child's environment is not nearly as powerful as guiding the child to make sense of the forms and functions of print. These activities will help children expand their awareness of print in the world around them through authentic and meaningful experiences:

- Encourage your child to play with toys such as alphabet blocks and magnetic letters because these toys provide opportunities to manipulate letters in a fun way.

- Point out environmental print on restaurant signs and menus, food containers, or signs on the street and draw attention to the fact that the letters and words help readers to understand what the signs and labels say.

- Consider creating labels for concrete and important items around the home. For example, help your children make signs with their names to hang on the doors of their rooms (Burns, Griffin, & Snow, 1999).

Justice (1998, 2000) report that while adults rarely reference print verbally (e.g., questions or comments about print) or nonverbally (e.g., tracking or pointing to print) without explicit instruction to do so, adults significantly increase their references to print with a minimal amount of instruction. Furthermore, when adults reference print during storybook reading sessions, children also ask more questions and make more comments about print (Ezell & Justice, 2000), and they show marked improvement in important early literacy abilities over a short period of time (Justice & Ezell, 2002). By talking about print within the interactive reading context, adults can make literacy an *explicit* rather than *implicit* focus in the reading routine.

Interactive Reading Activities
for Building Print Knowledge

Adults can intentionally target print knowledge during shared reading with children to encourage children's achievements in print knowledge. Here we present activities using specific storybooks and strategies that can assist children in developing print knowledge. Activities are arranged in a developmental sequence to enable children to achieve the following objectives:

1. To comprehend and begin to use print-related vocabulary
2. To demonstrate awareness of book organization
3. To understand the role of words as carrying meaning
4. To demonstrate understanding of text directionality
5. To demonstrate word awareness

ACTIVITY 2.1

Words About Print

Objective: To comprehend and begin to use print-related vocabulary

Storybook: *I Went Walking* (1990) by Sue Williams, illustrated by Julie Vivas

Description: *I Went Walking* uses simple, short sentences and contains just one sentence per page. The text is predictable because of its repetition and support from the illustrations (e.g., part of an animal is shown to provide a clue about what the next animal will be). The sentence forms alternate between statements and questions throughout the story, with the final sentence ending in an exclamation. The variety of sentences provides an excellent context to draw attention to varying sentence forms, how they are punctuated, and how they sound when read aloud. The repetitive text allows children to quickly become familiar with new vocabulary and concepts.

An important early print accomplishment is learning the language of storybooks, particularly the use of a *metalinguistic, print-focused* vocabulary. This vocabulary provides the child with the tools for talking about print and analyzing written language. This includes words such as *cover, title, author, illustrator, letter, page, word, sentence, front, back, beginning,* and *end*.

Interactive Reading Experience Using *I Went Walking*

Text	Extratextual Conversation
(cover, pp. 1–4)	
I Went Walking WRITTEN BY *Sue Williams* ILLUSTRATED BY *Julie Vivas*	Adult: Let's look at the *front* of the book. This is called the *cover* of the book. The name of the book is right here [points to title]. *I Went Walking* is the title. The person who wrote the book is

called the *author*. Her name is right here [points to author's name]—Sue Williams. There is another name here [points to illustrator's name]—Julie Vivas. She is the *illustrator*, the person who drew the pictures.

I went walking.
What did you see?

Adult: The *first* word on this page is *I*. And here is the second word, *went*.

The preceding extratextual conversation illustrates the use of strategies that include pointing to text and making comments related to print vocabulary. These may help to increase the child's awareness and understanding of these print-related concepts. Also notice that the preceding conversation simply draws attention to features of the book and models the corresponding vocabulary. No demand is made on the child to participate beyond attending to the adult's comments.

Words From Start to Finish

Objective: To demonstrate awareness of book organization

Storybook: *If You Give a Moose a Muffin* (1991) by Laura Numeroff, illustrated by Felicia Bond

Description: This book features a colorful cover that clearly displays the title, author's name, and illustrator's name. The story line follows a friendly moose who, when you give him one thing, always wants something else to go with it. The sequence of the story lends itself to predicting what comes next and requires that each page be explored before going on to the subsequent one.

If You Give a Moose a Muffin has some unique features that make it particularly appropriate for increasing awareness of book organization. The inviting illustrations of the friendly moose participating in familiar activities (e.g., eating muffins, painting, cleaning up a mess) are sure to engage children. Beginning with the cover, adults have opportunities to draw children's attention to print, for example, by pointing to the title, author's name, and the illustrator's name. The primary goals are to convey concepts related to the organization of books, such as the following:

- The front of the book is called the cover and tells us the title and the author.
- Starting at the front of the book, we turn one page at a time.

Interactive Reading Experience Using *If You Give a Moose a Muffin*

Text	Extratextual Conversation
(pp. 1–5)	
[Hand the book to the child in a random direction—with the spine or back of the book facing toward him or her.]	Adult: I need to start reading at the front of the book. Show me where I should start reading. Child: [points to the cover]
If you give a moose a muffin,	Adult: [opens book to first page] Where should I start reading on this page? [If necessary, adult gives the child choices by pointing first to the word *If*, then to *moose*, and then asks which one to start with.]
he'll want some jam to go with it. [pause for comment]	Adult: I finished reading this page [points to the page on the left]. Now, where should I read next?
So you'll bring out some of your mother's homemade blackberry jam.	Child: [points to right-hand page or first line of text on that page]

Note that to increase children's awareness of book organization, the adult incorporates the print-related vocabulary and concepts from the previous activity and then shifts to increasingly involved and advanced forms of these concepts. As children become more skilled at employing these concepts, educators can require higher levels of accuracy in children's responses and participation. For example, in the last question by the adult in the previous extratextual conversation ("Now, where should I read next?"), children may initially just point to the page on the right. With more practice and modeling of the vocabulary and concepts, one might expect the child to point to the first word in the first sentence on the right-hand page.

ACTIVITY 2.3

The Story Is in the Words

Objective: To understand the role of words as carrying meaning

Storybook: *Growing Vegetable Soup* (1987) by Lois Ehlert

Description: This book features illustrations in bold colors and a story written in large, salient print. In addition to the story text, print is used to label illustrations on each page. The story moves step-by-step through planting, growing, harvesting, preparing, and eating the vegetables grown in a garden and includes instructions on how to make your own vegetable soup.

Adults can draw attention to the role of print as having meaning using two simple types of print-referencing techniques:

1. Nonverbal references, such as pointing to words or tracking words when reading
2. Verbal references, such as commenting on print (e.g., "There's a picture of the sun. Look, these letters next to it spell the word *sun*.")

Initially, the adults should simply model print concepts for children and draw attention to the print through verbal and nonverbal references. Later, when a book becomes familiar, adults should encourage children to take a more active role in identifying print.

Interactive Reading Experience Using *Growing Vegetable Soup*

Text	Extratextual Conversation
(pp. 1–7)	
We're ready to work, and our tools are ready, too.	Adult: There's a picture of the tools. I see a shovel [points to the picture], and right above it are the letters that make the word *shovel* [points to the label]. (This can be repeated with the other tools in the picture.)
We are planting the seeds,	Adult: These words help to tell the story, so I will read them [points to the words and follows along with a finger while reading]: "We-are-planting-the-seeds."
And all the sprouts,	Adult: Look, all the sprouts have their names on them [points out the labels on each picture]. Here it says, "tomato sprout, pepper sprout, and cabbage sprout."

As the child becomes more familiar with a book and the words in the story, adults can make tasks more challenging. For example, adults can point to the picture of the shovel and ask, "What do you think this word above the shovel says?" At this point, children will still benefit from the support of the picture, which will assist them in building awareness and understanding of the correspondence between words and pictures. To increase the challenge, adults might point out the first occurrence of the word *grow* on one page and then ask children to "find another word that looks the same" as the target word.

ACTIVITY 2.4

Show Me the Words

Objective: To demonstrate understanding of text directionality

Storybook: *Mama Cat Has Three Kittens* (1998) by Denise Fleming

Description: This is a story of two kittens who follow Mama Cat's lead and one kitten who aims to be different than his siblings. The large print and clear organization of text (one to three short lines of text per page) make this book an appropriate choice for drawing attention to the text and the order in which we read the words.

Previously, we discussed the use of nonverbal print-referencing strategies (tracking and pointing to print) to help the child distinguish print from pictures while reading. Once children understand that words (as well as pictures) tell the story, they are likely able to examine more closely how to approach the text when reading, such as where to start and in which direction to move across the page.

Interactive Reading Experience Using *Mama Cat Has Three Kittens*

Text	Extratextual Conversation
(pp. 1–5)	
Mama Cat has three kittens, Fluffy, Skinny, and Boris.	Adult: [following along with a finger, points to the text as it is read] Look, I just read these words at the bottom of the page. I started over here. It says [rereads the sentence while again tracking with a finger].
When Mama Cat washes her paws,	Adult: This page has two lines of words, so I will read the top one first [points to the top line of text].
Fluffy and Skinny wash their paws. [at top of page] *Boris naps.* [at bottom of page]	Adult: Look, there are words at the top and bottom of this page. Which ones do you think I will read first?

[Child may point to the words or say "at the top."]

Adult: [regardless of the correctness of the child's response] I will start up here [points to first line of text] at the top of the page and read this line first.

In the preceding extratextual conversation, the adult draws attention to the directionality of print with verbal and nonverbal print-referencing strategies. When adults first introduce this concept to children, making extratextual comments after reading each and every sentence can be distracting and take away from the enjoyment of the story, so verbal references should be minimized early on. However, tracking print visually with a finger is less intrusive and may be appropriate on each page. In a book such as *Mama Cat*, incorporating comments and questions every two to three pages would still provide at least five opportunities throughout the book to make comments about print.

After providing several verbal and nonverbal print references, including tracking the print when reading, the adult can consider involving the child in some of these print-referencing strategies. For example, the child can be provided choices for where to begin reading on the page, such as "Should I start reading here," [points to first word on the page] "or here?" [points to last word on the page]. These choices serve as a scaffold for children, with the eventual goal being for them to identify the starting and ending points on the page independently.

Word Search

Objective: To demonstrate word awareness

Storybook: *Brown Bear, Brown Bear, What Do You See?* (1967/1992) by Bill Martin Jr, illustrated by Eric Carle

Description: This book features simple, repetitive text that children can memorize with ease. Clear, bright pictures of the animals support the text that changes on each page. When children are able to name pictures with little or no effort, adults should then move to a focus on word-to-print relationships.

The goal of this activity is to begin to highlight words in print. Children may not naturally recognize that sentences are made up of separate words and thus benefit from cues that help them attend to words as specific units of print. The repetitive text in this particular book gives children opportunities to see the same words several times throughout the story (e.g., *brown, bear, see*).

Interactive Reading Experience Using *Brown Bear, Brown Bear, What Do You See?*

Text	Extratextual Conversation
Brown Bear, *Brown Bear,* *What do you see?*	Adult: I heard the word *bear* two times in that sentence. Here is the first one [points to the first *bear* in the sentence]. You find another word that looks the same.
Red Bird, *Red Bird,* *What do you see?*	Adult: What animal do you see on this page? [allows time for the child to respond] Let's find the word that names this animal [helps the child find the word *bird*].
Yellow Duck, *Yellow Duck,* *What do you see?*	Adult: The word *see* is the last word on this page. Which word do you think is the word *see*? [helps the child find the last word, *see*]

This familiar storybook also lends itself to pretend reading, described in the introduction of this chapter. Adults should encourage children who have memorized the text in a storybook such as *Brown Bear* to attend to specific words in print and match them to the words they hear. This will help the child gain confidence in storybook interactions and help to develop the true ability to read text.

Additional Storybooks for Building Print Knowledge

Come Along, Daisy! (1998) by Jane Simmons

Daisy Duck is very curious and likes to explore on her own. As she wanders away, Mama Duck calls, "Come along, Daisy!" but Daisy doesn't listen. When she gets a little too far away, Daisy gets scared and calls for Mama Duck. Bright illustrations will engage young readers, as will the familiar notion of children testing boundaries. This is a good book for talking about print vocabulary, book organization, and text directionality.

Don't Let the Pigeon Drive the Bus (2003) by Mo Willems

This silly and entertaining book about a pigeon who wants to drive a bus will engage readers of all ages. At the outset, the bus driver assigns the reader the responsibility of watching the bus and not letting the pigeon drive the bus. The entire text of the book is written in speech bubbles to represent the bus driver and pigeon talking. This feature makes this an excellent book for print awareness activities and is particularly useful to convey the role of print in carrying meaning.

Fall Leaves Fall! (2000) by Zoe Hall, illustrated by Shari Halpern

Two brothers wait for fall each year so that they can collect, rake, and jump in the colorful leaves that fall off the trees. Near the end of the story, the boys make leaf pictures and label each type of leaf. This illustration offers a print-salient context in which to talk about the letters next to the leaves that spell their names. This book can thus be used to demonstrate the role of words as conveying meaning. This is a great book for the fall season when children can collect leaves, make pictures, and label them with the appropriate names.

Good Night, Gorilla (1994) by Peggy Rathmann

The zookeeper says goodnight to each of the zoo animals, who he believes are locked up safely for the night...but the gorilla has other ideas. This book uses simple, repetitive text (the words *good* and *night* appear on almost every page), which allows children to become quickly familiar with the words on the page.

If You Give a Mouse a Cookie (1985) by Laura Numeroff, illustrated by Felicia Bond

Written with the same flow as *If You Give a Moose a Muffin* (Numeroff, 1991), this story is one of a mischievous mouse who asks for milk to go with his cookie. That milk gives him a milk mustache, and the adventure begins! This is an excellent book for reinforcing print vocabulary and focusing on book organization.

My Car (2001) by Byron Barton

A book illustrated in bold colors, this is a story of Sam, his car, and how he takes care of it and uses it. It includes some pages with embedded print such as the gas pump, street signs, and the city bus route. But don't put this book down before reading the last page, because a car is not the only thing that Sam drives.

My Street (1998) by Rebecca Treays, illustrated by Rachel Wells

Milly and Jack tell about the streets that they live on, including what is under the street, how long their streets are, and the other buildings that are on their streets. The text in this book is abundant, which may be overwhelming for some young readers; however, the excellent use of text to label the actions and places Milly and Jack encounter makes this book useful for increasing word knowledge. Print is also embedded in the pictures (e.g., the words *POST OFFICE* displayed on the front of the post office building), which provides another opportunity to draw attention to print.

Sheep in a Jeep (1986) by Nancy Shaw, illustrated by Margot Apple

The novelty of this story will keep children interested to the final page. For starters, who has ever seen sheep drive a jeep? The antics of these sheep driving the jeep, getting stuck in the mud, then finally getting out, only to face a final mishap, make this book a page turner for young children. This book has relatively few words and few lines of words on each page, making it suitable for drawing attention to print, left-to-right movement, and top-to-bottom progression. The repetition of the words *sheep* and *jeep* also makes this book appropriate for word-finding activities.

Spot Goes to the Farm (1987) by Eric Hill

The always curious Spot explores the farm with his dad, looking for some baby animals. This is a lift-the-flap book, which allows children to interact directly with the book and become engaged in guessing what Spot will find next. With lots of questions and exclamations in the text, it is a good book for highlighting the differences in sentence endings and the expressions to match them. Bubbles of speech are present on most pages, representing the animals' noises or words and highlighting the fact that the animals are "talking."

We're Going on a Bear Hunt (1992) by Michael Rosen, illustrated by Helen Oxenbury

Be a part of the excitement as a family of four children and their father goes on a bear hunt. Each environment they pass through on their hunt inspires its own sound effect, which children love to imitate (the long, wavy grass goes "Swishy swashy! Swishy swashy! Swishy swashy!" as they go through it). No one is scared until they come upon that bear! Then the whole family must travel back through each environment before making it to the safety of home! This book is appropriate for drawing attention to a variety of punctuation at the ends of sentences. There are several lines of text per page, so this could also be used in a more challenging task to address top-to-bottom and left-to-right directionality.

The strategies in this chapter emphasize adults' use of a print-related vocabulary as children learn to attend to book organization, the role of words as carrying meaning, text directionality, and words as units of print. Through adults deliberately exposing children to conventions of books and print, children are likely to begin to value print as an object worthy of their attention and will feel comfortable discussing print as they work actively with adults by turning pages and tracking print with their finger. Chapter 3, on building word knowledge, provides adults with strategies for increasing children's vocabulary in more general ways so that they can talk not only about what the title of their favorite book is but also about how their favorite book makes them think and feel.

Building Word Knowledge: Increasing the Complexity of Words Children Understand and Produce

For children, *word knowledge* means understanding and using words of different form classes—including nouns, verbs, adjectives, and adverbs—and having a word repertoire for precisely representing thoughts, needs, interests, and ideas. Children's precision increases from toddlerhood through adulthood as their word knowledge develops: For instance, an object is first described as *big*, later as *large*, then *gigantic*, and finally as *monstrous*. Although *big, large, gigantic,* and *monstrous* mean more or less the same thing, these word variations give children greater precision in representing their thoughts. Beyond enabling a child's self-expression, word knowledge is closely linked to reading comprehension, and children who have better word knowledge are able to focus their cognitive resources on other aspects of the reading process, such as linking new concepts to known concepts (NICHD, 2000b).

How Word Knowledge Develops

Word knowledge begins to develop from a very early age. Children typically produce their first true word by the time they are 1 year old, and their vocabulary size increases to about 50 words by 18 months of age. At 18 months, when children have accrued an expressive vocabulary of about 50 words, they enter a "vocabulary explosion" (e.g., Goldfield & Reznick, 1990) until about 24 months, during which their vocabulary can grow at a rate of as many as 9 new words per day (cf. Ganger & Brent, 2004). Vocabulary growth continues through the preschool, elementary school, and high school years so that by the time children graduate, they will have learned about 60,000 words (Pinker, 1994). Children learn most words without explicit instruction in nonostensive contexts, including overhearing, and through social interactions with others. Because the language children experience in the world around them contributes greatly to the amount and type of word learning, considerable variation exists in children's word knowledge (e.g., Hart & Risley, 1995; Hoff & Naigles, 2002). Building a solid foundation of concepts and the words that label them *before* children enter school is crucial because children have an easier time learning new words if they already have several words under their belt. In other words, children with larger vocabularies tend to learn new words with relative ease, and children with smaller vocabularies learn new words more slowly by comparison. This occurs because children refine the semantic representations of words they know and create relationships between new words and known words (Snow et al., 1998). Even at the youngest ages, the ability to understand and remember the meanings of new words depends strongly on how well developed a child's vocabulary already is (Robbins & Ehri, 1994).

One context that has been well studied for its role in teaching children new words is that of interactive book reading. Research on word learning uses storybook reading as a vehicle for understanding children's novel word learning because it can be controlled easily. For instance, a researcher can read a book with children several times and study how many new words they learn from the activity. Numerous studies have used this approach, which has provided several interesting facts about the development of word knowledge through interactive reading (e.g., Elley, 1989; Justice, Meier, & Walpole, 2005; Nagy, Anderson, & Herman, 1987; Penno et al., 2002; see also NICHD, 2000a). First, children's acquisition of a new word moves from a broad, shallow understanding to greater specificity and deepened understanding over time with ongoing exposures to that word in different contexts. Second, the more often children hear a word in text, the more likely they are to learn it. Children learn words more readily when they occur several times in a single book and when they hear a word in repeated readings of the same book. Only hearing a word once or twice is not always sufficient for acquisition. Third, metalinguistic discussions about words when they occur in texts enable children's learning of words, and this learning is further supported when children have the opportunities to use words in drama or other book-related activities that supplement hearing the word in text. In short, although being exposed to a novel word in a single storybook reading is useful for developing children, educators can accelerate children's word learning by allowing them to hear new words many times in varying circumstances. Helping parents to support their children's word knowledge in the home environment is an important goal of early education. On the next page, we provide some tips for parents that may promote word learning in the home environment.

How Interactive Reading Supports the Development of Word Knowledge

Storybook reading interactions provide valuable opportunities for children to be exposed to and learn new words. The language contained within storybook readings is

word KnowLeDGe tiPs for parents

Parents can build their children's word knowledge by making a few simple adjustments to the way they speak to their children. The following are strategies proposed by Weitzman and Greenberg (2002) that parents can incorporate into their interactions with children:

- *Wait and Listen*—Encourage your child to initiate verbally by waiting expectantly for her initiations. Be comfortable with long pauses during conversations. When your child does take turns in conversations, allow him the time to make complete responses.

- *Follow Your Child's Lead*—Talk about what your child wants to talk about. Focus conversations with your child on her topic of attention, not yours.

- *Be Face to Face*—Adjust your physical level so that you are on the same level as your child when conversing and playing.

- *Avoid Test Questions and Yes/No Questions*—Use open-ended questions to which you do not know the answer (e.g., "Why do you think the boy is crying?") rather than test questions (questions you know the answer to, such as "What color is that?") and yes/no questions (questions requiring a yes or no response, such as "Do you want to read this book?").

- *Expand*—Repeat your child's words and add a few additional ideas or concepts (e.g., Child: That a bear. Mother: That is a big grizzly bear).

exceptionally rich and provides words and grammar that do not often occur in the conversations that happen at home and in classrooms. When adults talk to children during book reading, they themselves use a more diverse array of syntax and vocabulary and a higher level of abstraction than in other language contexts, such as playing with toys (Sorsby & Martlew, 1991). Storybook reading also provides a context through which children gain oral language and literacy skills in an integrated manner, whereby children can learn new words as they develop print knowledge and phonological awareness (Snow et al., 1998).

When prereaders listen to books and when readers read books, their comprehension of that text places a high demand on vocabulary knowledge. At the same time, when children encounter new words and must infer meaning and retain new words for future comprehension, their ability to do so is strongly dependent on their background knowledge of other words and concepts (e.g., NICHD, 2000b). In the toddler, preschool, and elementary school years, educators are encouraged to give children a leg up on reading by introducing children to as many different words as possible. In doing so, educators should recognize that children's learning of new words does not need to follow any specific developmental timeline. For instance, children do not need to learn the word *big* before they can learn *large*. As a general rule of thumb, children are ready to learn any new word if they can handle the underlying concept—thus, once a child understands the concept of *bigness* she can handle the different words that describe bigness (e.g., *big, large, huge, humongous*, etc.). This is why a 2-year-old child with an interest in trains is capable of rapidly acquiring a train lexicon to include *steam engine, locomotive, caboose, hopper car, smokestack, tender car*, and so forth. The child's emerging lexicon for these words and others is constrained by only two features: (1) the extent to which the child understands the underlying concept represented by a word (e.g., *steam engine* versus *liberty*) and (2) the extent to which the child has exposure to the word within his word-learning environment.

Interactive Reading Activities for Building Word Knowledge

Here we present storybooks and interactive strategies designed to foster children's word knowledge. Activities address the following objectives:

1. To understand and use verbs and verb morphology
2. To interpret the intentions underlying action verbs
3. To use words to express emotions and other mental concepts
4. To understand and use adjectives
5. To differentiate and use prepositions and other opposites

Attention to Action

Objective: To understand and use verbs and verb morphology

Storybook: *Mr. Gumpy's Outing* (1970) by John Burningham

Description: This book describes a boat ride adventure that Mr. Gumpy embarks upon along with several animals and children. Mr. Gumpy warns all of the passengers that they must behave, by instructing each of them to refrain from a particular action that could be dangerous if performed on the boat. Many different verbs are introduced throughout the story, using varied verb morphology, including *to kick, to trample, to flap, to bleat*, and more.

This activity focuses on action verbs and verb morphology. Teaching children about actions, activities, events, and the words that label them is important because action verbs are arguably more difficult for children to learn than concrete object nouns (Gentner, 1978, 1982; Imai, Haryu, & Okada, 2002). In addition to the conceptual complexities surrounding verbs, children must master the morphology of verbs so as to express their thoughts with accuracy. For example, to describe an action that is in progress, we use the morpheme *-ing* (e.g., the dog is *running* around the yard), and to express a completed action, we use the morpheme *-ed* (e.g., I *painted* a picture in school today), or some irregular verb form, which must be memorized (e.g., The dog *ran* around the yard). Readers will notice in the activity that adults can introduce novel action verbs and their accompanying morphology using strategies that do not resemble the grammar lessons that many adults remember.

Interactive Reading Experience Using *Mr. Gumpy's Outing*

Text	Extratextual Conversation
(pp. 18–22)	
"Can you make room for me?" said the calf. *"Yes, if you don't trample about."*	Adult: Mr. Gumpy doesn't want the calf to *trample* about. That means he doesn't want the calf to step on everything while he is on the boat. What else *tramples* on things? What kinds of things might a dog *trample* on?
"May I join you, Mr. Gumpy?" *said the goat.* *"Very well, but don't kick."*	Adult: Mr. Gumpy is afraid the goat might *kick* someone. I bet it hurts when a goat *kicks*. Can you think of some times when it is good to *kick*? I like *kicking* the soccer ball around the yard.
For a little while they all went along happily but then…The goat kicked, the calf trampled, the chickens flapped…	Adult: Oh no! The chickens started *flapping*. Do you know what it looks like for a chicken to *flap* its wings? When a chicken *flaps* its wings, it looks like this [bends arms at the elbows and flaps arms like a chicken]. Can you show me how you would *flap* your wings? Child: [demonstrates flapping action]

Mr. Gumpy's Outing is an excellent book for introducing new action verbs to children using multiple syntactic frames. Notice that in the extratextual conversation the adult highlights and fosters an understanding of the actions and activities taking place in the story by labeling and defining them, repeating the verbs that label the actions, using the verbs that label actions in multiple syntactic frames (e.g., *kick, kicks, kicking*), demonstrating the actions and having the child perform those actions, and by asking the child questions about the actions. All of these strategies should be beneficial for assisting children in mapping novel verbs to actions (Pence, 2004).

Why We Do the Things We Do

Objective: To interpret the intentions underlying action verbs

Storybook: *The Very Busy Spider* (1984) by Eric Carle

Description: This colorful and cheerfully illustrated book describes an active day in the life of a spider blown onto a farmyard fence where she begins to spin a web. Barnyard animal friends visit the busy spider throughout the day and invite her to join them in various activities, but the spider, intent on spinning her web, doesn't respond and continues working on her creation. One special feature of this book is the raised spider web on each page. Children will enjoy following the trail with their fingers as it grows from a single line into a complex and beautiful web. Many different verbs are introduced throughout the story, including *to blow, to land, to spin, to go for a ride, to eat, to run, to jump, to roll, to chase, to take a nap, to go for a swim, to catch, to build,* and *to answer.*

This activity encourages children to interpret the intentions underlying actions, including how to think about action–result sequences, how to differentiate purposeful and accidental actions, and how to interpret the goals of others. Children's understanding of the goal-directedness of actions, for example, helps them to develop the ability to understand others' intentions (Woodward, Sommerville, & Guajardo, 2001). Children learn about goal-directed actions via their observations of actions, by performing actions themselves, and through their social interactions with others (Woodward, 1999). In this activity, the adult initiates discussion about the intentions underlying actions.

Interactive Reading Experience Using *The Very Busy Spider*

Text	Extratextual Conversation
(pp. 1–3)	
Early one morning the wind blew a spider across the field. A thin, silky thread trailed	Adult: This says, "The spider *landed* on a fence post." This is what it would look

from her body. The spider landed on a fence post near a farm yard...

like for a spider to *land* on a fence [moves hand with fingers spread to look like a spider landing on outstretched arm]. The spider is so light that the wind just carried her to the fence post. It was an accident because the spider didn't choose to *land* on the fence. Sometimes accidents can be good, right?

And began to spin a web with her silky thread.

Adult: The spider is *spinning* a web. That means she is making a web with her silk. Why do you think she's *spinning* a web?

Adult: See how the silky thread comes out of the spider's body? See if you can trace the web with your finger [moves child's finger along the web if necessary]. See how she moved from this fence post to that fence post?

In the extratextual conversation about *The Very Busy Spider*, note that the adult encourages the child to think about actions and activities and does not simply ask the child to repeat words and their definitions. The adult also takes advantage of the opportunity to facilitate the child's understanding of action–result sequences (the spider's action was spinning her silk, and the result was a beautiful web) and goals or intentions or actions (the spider spun a web so that she could catch flies to eat).

ACTIVITY 3.3

Talking About Feelings

Objective: To use words to express emotions and other mental concepts

Storybook: *A to Z, Do You Ever Feel Like Me? A Guessing Alphabet of Feelings, Words, and Other Cool Stuff* (1999) by Bonnie Hausman, photography by Sandi Fellman

Description: This book presents a rhyming riddle containing a different emotion for each letter of the alphabet. For each emotion, the author presents a situation in which the reader might experience that emotion as well as objects beginning with that same letter. For example, the riddle for letter *S* says, "I went into the haunted house because I was dared. But it was too dark and spooky, and now I'm s_____." Some of the other objects on the page beginning with the target letter are *starfish, seahorses, stamps, shovels, snakes, skateboards,* and *spoons.*

This activity introduces children to specific words that they can use to express emotions and mental concepts. Emotions and mental concepts are difficult for children to grasp because they are not tangible and cannot be observed directly. Introducing children to the labels for emotions and mental concepts empowers them to express themselves in socially appropriate ways and to communicate their feelings unambiguously using words. Readers may have observed how some children suddenly withdraw from a conversation or social situation when they do not possess the vocabulary to express that they have been upset or embarrassed, for example. Even worse, children who are unable to express their emotions using words might cry or use physical means to convey their feelings (e.g., a child throws a temper tantrum when he doesn't want to leave his grandmother's house). Young children who are equipped with the language to express their feelings and emotional states can resolve conflicts with peers and family members directly before a pleasant situation escalates to an unpleasant one.

Interactive Reading Experience Using A to Z, Do You Ever Feel Like Me?

Text
(page for letter A)

Extratextual Conversation

When my sister takes my stuff without asking first, I could just scream. This morning I found my bow on her teddy bear. I know she's little, but sometimes she makes me so _____.

Adult: How do you feel when your sister takes your things?
Child: I share with her.
Adult: You're right. You do share with her and that is very nice of you. Does she ever take your things without asking?
Child: Yeah. Sometimes she does.
Adult: How do you feel when she takes your toys without asking first?
Child: I get mad!
Adult: That's right, you feel angry.

The first few times reading this book with a child, the adult will probably have to provide the target words for the child. When reading, the adult can ask the children to describe times when they might feel each of the emotions. It may be that they have not experienced some of the emotions themselves, but they might be able to tell about someone else who has. The adult might also have the children try to imitate the emotion depicted on each of the pages as the adult reinforces them (e.g., "Wow, you do look angry!") or ask the children to tell what they might say when angry (e.g., "It makes me angry when you take my toys!").

Enhancing Language With Descriptive Words

Objective: To understand and use adjectives

Storybook: *They Call Me Woolly: What Animal Names Can Tell Us* (2002) by Keith DuQuette

Description: This book introduces children to animals and their names. As the book explains, animal names are often very revealing. Some animal names give clues about where those animals are from, as is the case for the *American alligator*. Other animal names show what animals like to eat, such as the bee-eater, or what their fur is like, as is true for the *woolly monkey*. Adults and older children will likely enjoy reading the interesting facts about each of the animals, located at the back of the book.

This activity focuses on adjectives. An adjective is a part of speech that modifies a noun (e.g., *brown* bear, *tall* man). When we think of adjectives, descriptive words including colors, sizes, and other physical attributes come to mind. During interactive reading with children, parents and educators often label objects for children but do not focus on the attributes of those objects (e.g., Choi, 2000; Choi & Gopnik, 1995). However, because preschoolers are equipped with some basic word-learning assumptions, or assumptions that allow them to draw inferences about the meanings of new words, adults familiar with these assumptions can capitalize on them when teaching preschoolers new words. One way that children infer the meanings of new words is by recruiting syntactic cues that signal a novel word's form class (e.g., noun, verb, adjective) to narrow the possibilities for that word's referent. For example, children who hear "This is an *X*" interpret *X* to be a *count noun*, while children who hear "This is *X*" interpret *X* to be a *proper name*, and children who hear "This is an *X* one" interpret *X* to be an *adjective* (Hall, Burns, & Pawluski, 2003). Children are also more likely to assume that a novel word is an adjective when it is applied to more than one object because count nouns and proper names rarely take more than a single label (Hall, 1996). Adults can make the most of these word-learning assumptions by structuring word-learning situations with preschoolers accordingly.

Interactive Reading Experience Using *They Call Me Woolly: What Animal Names Can Tell Us*

Text	Extratextual Conversation
(pp. 1–3)	
Blue-tongued or burrowing, woolly or whooping, there's so much to discover in an animal's name.	Adult: This book is going to teach us about a lot of different animals. All of the animals in this book have special

names. The animals' names tell us something about the animals, like where they live, what they eat, or what they look like.

A name can tell you where an animal is from: the **African elephant** *and the* **American alligator***.*

Adult: This is an *African elephant*. Where do you think the *African* elephant is from? *African* elephants are from Africa. You can tell by their name.

Adult: Do you know anything else that has *African* in its name? *African Americans* are people who have family that lived in Africa at one time.

Or it can tell you about the animal's habitat: the **polar bear** *and the* **mountain goat***.*

Adult: The *polar* bear's name tells us that the *polar* bear lives near the North Pole where it is very cold and icy.

Adult: What does the mountain goat's name tell us about it? What else has *mountain* in its name? Mountain *lions* have mountain in their name because they also live in the mountains.

Notice that all of the animal names in *They Call Me Woolly* are in boldface type. While reading, the adult can comment on the adjectives and explain how each one provides hints about what the animal is like. If possible, the adult can take advantage of preschoolers' word-learning assumptions when teaching them adjectives by using the construction "This is an *X* one" and by using the same adjective to describe multiple objects.

On the Contrary

Objective: To differentiate and use prepositions and other opposites

Storybook: *How Big Is a Pig?* (2000) by Clare Beaton, illustrated by Stella Blackstone

Description: This book introduces children to opposites, including some prepositions, using pictures of barnyard animals that appear to be sewn onto the pages. Each page presents animal opposites in a rhyming format and repeats the question "But how big is a pig?" The opposites of interest include *thin/fat, quick/slow, in/out, jumpy/still, wild/tame, high/low, dirty/clean, young/old, black/white,* and *big/small.*

This activity focuses on prepositions and other opposites. Prepositions are words such as *at*, *by*, *with*, and *from* that link nouns and pronouns to another word in a sentence. As adults, we tend to overestimate preschoolers' understanding of prepositions. While children begin to use some prepositions, such as *in* and *on*, between 28 and 36 months (Brown, 1973), they do not use others, including temporal prepositions (e.g., *before*, *after*) until they are much older. When younger children use these prepositions, they may confuse them with similar concepts. In this activity, we have grouped prepositions with opposite words because they can generally be contrasted with one another in word-learning situations in the same way that opposites can. For example, *under* can be contrasted with *over*, and *to* can be contrasted with *from* to convey the meanings of both of these words. The adult can guide children to differentiate and use prepositions and other opposites in shared reading.

Interactive Reading Experience Using *How Big Is a Pig?*

Text	Extratextual Conversation
(pp. 1–3)	
Some cows are thin; some cows are fat. But how big is a pig? Can you tell me that?	Adult: Let's look at these two cows: One is *thin*, and the other is *fat*. Do you think the pig is *thin* or *fat*? That's right. The pig is *fat*.
	Adult: What kinds of animals are *fat*? *Whales* and *elephants* are *fat*. What kinds of animals are *thin*? *Snakes* and *worms* are *thin*.
	Adult: Can you think of another word that means the same thing as *thin*? *Skinny* means the same thing as *thin*. How about another word that means the same thing as *fat*? *Big* means almost the same as *fat*.
Some dogs are quick; some dogs are slow. But how big is a pig? Do you think you know?	Adult: Which one of these dogs looks *quick*, and which one looks *slow*? How do you know? This dog [on the right page] is *quick*. We can tell because it looks like he's running. This dog [on the left page] is *slow*. We know because he looks like he is walking.

Adult: Do you think the pig is *quick* or *slow*? This is a *slow* pig. What other animals are *slow*? Turtles and snails are *slow*. What other animals are *quick*? Cheetahs and rabbits are *quick* because they can run very fast.

Adult: Do you know another word that means the same thing as *quick*? Fast means the same thing as *quick*. How about another word that means the same thing as *slow*? *Sluggish* means almost the same thing as *slow* because slugs are *slow* animals.

Some hens are in; some hens are out. But how big is a pig? What's this all about?

Adult: How many hens are *in*? Right, four hens are *in*. How many hens are *out*? Yes, five hens are *out*.

Adult: When it rains, would you rather be *in* or *out*? How come?

Adult: What do you think the hens do when they are *out*? It looks like they search for worms to eat when they are *out*. What do you think the hens do when they are *in*? They must lay eggs when they are *in*.

In the preceding extratextual conversation, the adult uses a variety of interactive techniques, from simply modeling concepts for the child ("One is *thin*, and the other is *fat*") to examining the thought process for considering these novel concepts ("Can you think of another word that means the same thing as *thin*?"). The adult provides generous scaffolds to engage the child in conceptual considerations that seem beyond the child's immediate reach but not too difficult to be frustrating.

Additional Storybooks for Building Word Knowledge

The Berenstain Bears Ready, Get Set, Go! (1988) by Stan and Jan Berenstain

Animals gather around as the Berenstain Bears participate in a series of Olympic events until they finally tire themselves out and need a rest. This book is great for presenting action verbs as well as adjectives. Each event begins with an action ("Ready, get set, climb!") and then presents a series of adjectives to describe the performance of each of the participants in the event ("Papa climbs *high*. Brother climbs *higher*. Sister climbs *highest...High, higher, highest. Good, better, best.*" [emphasis added]).

Calico Cat at the Zoo (1981) by Donald Charles

A calico cat takes a trip to the zoo to visit the animals. While there, he describes each of the animals with a different adjective. The adjectives are presented in contrastive pairs (*shy/proud*), and each pair ends in a rhyming word (*shy/proud, quiet/loud*). The last page of the book has a picture of each of the animals the calico cat saw at the zoo, along with its name.

Elephants Aloft (1993) by Kathi Appelt, illustrated by Keith Baker

Elephants Rama and Raja travel in a hot-air balloon to see their Auntie Rwanda. Prepositions such as *above, through, behind,* and *across* are presented one per page as the two elephants journey from Asia to Africa. The illustrations in this book lend themselves well to presenting prepositions that might otherwise be hard for children to understand.

Exactly the Opposite (1990) by Tana Hoban

Exactly the Opposite contains no words beyond the title but includes several bright and interesting photographs of opposite images. Because there are no words, the reader is able to decide which aspect or aspects of each photograph to contrast. For example, the first page of the book depicts a pair of hands, one open and the other closed in a fist. The reader might also contrast the concepts of left and right using this same picture.

The Foot Book (1968/2002) by Dr. Seuss

The Foot Book is a brightly illustrated rhyming book all about feet. Opposites are used throughout the book to describe various foot attributes, including textures, sizes, colors, and much more. Opposites in this book are presented in ways that are funny and memorable.

How Are You Peeling? Foods With Moods (1999) by Saxton Freymann and Joost Elffers

A cornucopia of feelings and emotions are introduced in this rhyming book's brightly colored photographs. Instead of illustrating emotions using human actors, this book uses fruits and vegetables that have been carved into faces. The book presents a surprisingly lifelike display of emotions, including an *amused* green pepper, a *frustrated* orange, and a *surprised* apple. This book illustrates emotions in a light and fun manner and allows adults to discuss how facial expressions can be used to convey emotions.

Jiggle, Wiggle, Prance (1987) by Sally Noll

Jiggle, Wiggle, Prance presents animals performing 36 different actions. Action words are labeled in bold letters at the bottom of each page. Every other page ends in a verb that rhymes with the verb on the page before it.

Sometimes I'm Bombaloo (2002) by Rachel Vail, illustrated by Yumi Heo

In this book about how a child deals with anger, Katie Honors describes herself as a really good and happy kid who sometimes loses her temper. When Katie is angry, she is not herself: She is Bombaloo. Being Bombaloo is scary for Katie, but after some time out and love from her mother, Katie eventually apologizes and returns to her old self. This book is appropriate for talking about emotions because it illustrates emotions that a young child might experience and describes these emotions from a child's point of view, using language that a child might use.

Super, Super, Superwords (1989) by Bruce McMillan

Adjectives are used visually and grammatically to demonstrate the three degrees of comparison. First, the positive (*big*) illustration provides an initial point of reference. Second, the comparative (*bigger*) illustration relates two objects, persons, or concepts to one another. In the case of this book, the comparative illustration shows an increase in quality from the positive illustration. Third, the superlative (*biggest*) illustration compares three objects, persons, or ideas, providing the most extreme quality of the three.

Trucks, Trucks, Trucks (1999) by Peter Sis

Any child with an interest in construction equipment will enjoy this book. The pictures and verbs on each page tell the story of Matt, a young boy who is asked to clean up the trucks in his bedroom. As Matt picks up the trucks, he imagines himself with a life-size version of each of the trucks, performing a different maneuver with each one. Adults can highlight the action verbs presented on each of the pages.

The activities in this chapter target the child's understanding and production of verbs and verb morphology, intentions underlying action verbs, emotions and mental concepts, adjectives, and prepositions and opposites. Discussions resulting from these activities will undoubtedly foster children's interest in acquiring new labels for an increasingly abstract array of events and emotions, as well as linguistically challenging words such as prepositions, so that they can express themselves with greater precision. Chapter 4 addresses another area of development that educators may readily support during interactive shared reading: phonological knowledge, which describes the child's sensitivity to how sounds come together to form syllables, words, and phrases.

Building Phonological Knowledge: Developing a Sensitivity to Sound Units of Language

Before children enter formal reading instruction, an important precursory ability that helps them to succeed in that instruction is phonological awareness. *Phonological awareness* describes children's nonlexical sensitivity to the sound structure of spoken language (Schatschneider, Francis, Foorman, Fletcher, & Mehta, 1999; Stahl & Murray, 1994). Phonological awareness is *nonlexical* in that it requires children to focus on the sound structure of a word or syllable rather than attending to its lexical or semantic attributes. For instance, asked what rhymes with *pig* (a phonological task), the child must consider its sound structure rather than its meaning. Phonological awareness is also a *metalinguistic* skill, meaning that it requires children to concentrate on and talk about language as an object of scrutiny. Engaging in phonological tasks, such as rhyming or matching words on the basis of specific sounds (e.g., the first sound in a word), requires children to work at a metalinguistic level, which may ease their transition to other academic tasks that also require attention toward language.

How Phonological Knowledge Develops

Phonological awareness is one aspect of a child's broader phonological system, which was described in chapter 1 as part of the language system. As children develop their phonological system, they also begin to focus on how the sounds of speech are used to organize spoken and written language. This aspect of phonological development is phonological awareness, and it is a domain of development that integrates language and literacy. From birth, children begin to learn the sounds that constitute speech, and phonological awareness emerges sometime in the period between birth and kindergarten for most children. Although the major achievements in phonological awareness emerge in a fairly predictable and regular developmental sequence for most children, not all children reach these achievements at the same time. For instance, one of the earliest phonological awareness developments is recognizing that multisyllabic words can be broken into smaller units, or syllables (e.g., *multiply* is *mul-ti-ply*). Some children may achieve this understanding by 2 years, other children may achieve it at 4 years, and some may not achieve it until first grade through direct instruction. Children's achievements in phonological awareness are highly contingent upon children's high-quality and sensitive exposure to explicit, phonology-focused interactions with more capable peers, such as parents and teachers. These interactions might include listening to nursery rhymes, playing sound games, or being read books that feature salient phonological patterns. Within such interactions, children's phonological awareness is fostered by the adult, who explicitly and intentionally draws the child's attention to phonological patterns.

Phonological awareness progresses from an understanding of larger units of sound, such as whole words and syllables, to an understanding of smaller units of sound, such as phonemes (e.g., Carroll, Snowling, Hulme, & Stevenson, 2003; Goswami & Bryant, 1990). Around 2 years of age, many children begin to understand that the phonological (sound) structures of words are separate from their meanings. Many children are even able to detect and produce patterns of rhyme, as evidenced by their understanding of nursery rhymes. By the time children are 3 years of age, they also may become sensitive to alliteration, or the sharing of an initial phoneme across words and syllables (Justice & Schuele, 2004). Alliteration is incorporated in many children's books, including *Watch William Walk* by Ann Jonas (1997). Around 4 years of age, children may be able to understand that words are composed of syllables, and many are able to manipulate these syllables based on onset–rime distinctions. An *onset* contains all of the sounds in a syllable that precede the first vowel (e.g., *spr-* in *spring*), and a *rime* contains the first vowel sound in a syllable and all the sounds that follow it (e.g., *-ing* in *spring*). Eventually, children are able to represent words and syllables as comprising a series of discrete phonemes, at which point they are exhibiting *phonemic awareness*. Children with phonemic awareness can blend a series of phonemes to make a word and can segment a word into its constituent phonemes. Although children need not have phonemic awareness to be able to learn to read, children who have a reasonably well-developed sensitivity to the sound structure of language are better able to profit from beginning reading instruction than children without this sensitivity (Torgesen, Wagner, & Rashotte, 1994). Also, children who have problems acquiring phonological awareness will proceed more slowly in reading instruction in kindergarten and first grade, which may set the stage for a host of later literacy-related problems (Stothard, Snowling, Bishop, Chipchase, & Kaplan, 1998). Helping parents to support their children's phonological knowledge in the home environment is an important goal of early education. On the next page, we provide some tips for parents that can foster children's phonological awareness in the home environment.

PHONOLOGICAL KNOWLEDGE TIPS FOR PARENTS

Parents can help children build phonological awareness in almost any setting. The parent simply needs to draw the child's attention to the sounds that make up sentences, words, or syllables. For example, when driving in the car, parents can create phonological awareness games for children by having them look out the window to see if they can find things that rhyme, things that start with the same sound, and things that end with the same sound. Following are some examples to say to your child:

• "Let's look for things we see that rhyme with *bag*."

• "Let's look for things that start with a /b/ sound."

• "Let's look for things that end with a /p/ sound."

How Interactive Reading Supports the Development of Phonological Knowledge

For most children, adult–child storybook reading is a familiar routine that is comfortable, authentic, meaningful, and interesting to the child. When reading storybooks, children are implicitly exposed to a great many phonological concepts, particularly when they are read rhyming books or other books that feature phonological patterns (e.g., alliteration). For some children, this implicit exposure is sufficient to provoke the development of phonological awareness. For other children, however, implicit exposure during interactive reading is not enough to stimulate phonological learning; rather, explicit guidance in the phonological structure of language is needed (Bailey, 1989; Watkins & Bunce, 1996). In moving from an implicit to an explicit focus, the adult intentionally guides the child to view phonological concepts as interesting and warranting exploration. This takes the child beyond mere exposure to salient phonological rhythms (e.g., Hickory dickory dock, the mouse ran up the clock) to exploration and careful consideration of those concepts (e.g., "I think I heard a rhyme! *Dock* and *clock*. Hmm, what else rhymes with *dock* and *clock*? Let's think of some...").

Phonological awareness activities are easy to infuse into interactive reading sessions. While reading, adults can comment on sound patterns that they hear and can involve children by having them focus on sounds as well. The adult can scaffold

the child's interactions with sound units to support the child's phonological awareness at a level beyond what is possible independently. Strategies that appear particularly beneficial include modeling (e.g., "Those two words rhyme"), contrasting
(e.g., "These words rhyme, and these do not"), extending (e.g., "Both of those words
start with /b/. What letter makes the /b/ sound?"), and withdrawing support as
the child progresses (e.g., "You did this one last time. Do you remember the first
sound in 'fish'?") (e.g., Justice & Pullen, 2003; Skibbe, Behnke, & Justice, in press).

Interactive Reading Activities
for Building Phonological Knowledge

Here we present approaches to using interactive reading to help children develop
phonological awareness. Specifically, five activities are aligned to the following objectives that are arranged in a developmental sequence to model children's achievements in phonological awareness.

1. To segment sentences at the word level

2. To segment words into syllables and blend parts of words

3. To demonstrate rhyme awareness and rhyme production

4. To demonstrate awareness of and produce beginning sounds

5. To demonstrate awareness of and produce final sounds

These and other early phonological skills provide a foundation for children's
later reading ability (e.g., Bear, Invernizzi, Templeton, & Johnston, 2004). Children
need not work solely on one achievement until mastery. A child may not be able to
rhyme with total success (our third objective) yet still can engage in phonological
tasks that require greater sophistication, such as matching words on the basis of final sounds (our fifth objective). Children can engage in both easier and harder tasks
when adults provide scaffolding that is sensitive and supportive.

Taking Apart Sentences

Objective: To segment sentences at the word level

Storybook: *Busy, Busy Mouse* (2003) by Virginia Kroll, illustrated by Fumi Kosaka

Description: This story looks at the parallel activities of a mouse and a family
during the day and night. It has many short sentences, which makes it a great book
for introducing segmentation.

To encourage an interest in segmenting sentences, adults are encouraged to use the following techniques:

1. To comment on the length of sentences
2. To clap for each word of the sentence
3. To ask children to "say just a little bit of 'sentence'" (Fox & Routh, 1975) until children break the sentence down to the word level

Interactive Reading Experience Using *Busy, Busy Mouse*

Text (pp. 1–6)	Extratextual Conversation
Up comes the sun.	Adult: I can clap for all of the words in this sentence: "Up [clap] comes [clap] the [clap] sun [clap]." Wow! That's four different words.
Good morning, everyone.	Adult: Can you clap for all of the words in this sentence? I'll clap with you. "Good [clap] morning [clap], everyone [clap]."
Baby crying.	Adult: Can you say just a little bit of this sentence? Child: "Baby." Adult: Great! That's a word. *Crying* is a word, too. There are two words in this sentence, *baby* and *crying* [points to words while reading].
Eggs frying.	Adult: There are two words in this sentence, too! *Eggs* is a word, and *frying* is a word [points to words].
Clay smashing.	Adult: Can you clap for all of the words in this sentence? There are two words: "Clay [clap] smashing [clap]."
Blocks bashing.	Adult: Can you say just a little bit of this sentence? Child: "Blocks." Adult: Great! That's a word. *Bashing* is a word, too.

Segmenting sentences at the word level is one of the easier phonological awareness tasks for a child to master. In this activity, note how the adult explicitly scaffolds the child to engage with the sound structure of oral language during the shared reading interaction. The adult scaffolds the child's phonological awareness using a number of different approaches (e.g., clapping for words, talking about different words) to supply a multisensory experience for the child. For the most part, the adult models the phonological concepts for the child, giving exposure to phonological units (e.g., words) that the child may not attend to otherwise at a metalinguistic level.

What's in a Word?

Objective: To segment words into syllables and blend parts of words

Storybook: *If You Give a Pig a Pancake* (1998) by Laura Numeroff, illustrated by Felicia Bond

Description: This delightful story about the adventures of a pig and her caretaker features many good opportunities for segmenting and blending words.

If You Give a Pig a Pancake is an excellent storybook to encourage children's interest in the sounds of words. It includes compound words, such as *pancake*, that are made up of two separate words. Compound words make it easier for children to think about the separate parts of any one word. To encourage an interest in segmenting and blending words, adults are encouraged to use the following four techniques throughout the reading:

1. To comment on the parts of words
2. To clap out the different parts of words (e.g., *bu-bbles*)
3. To encourage children to say the parts of compound words separately (e.g., *homesick* without the *home*)
4. To help children combine syllables of words together (e.g., "*Pan* and *cake* are two little words. What happens when we put them together?")

Interactive Reading Experience Using *If You Give a Pig a Pancake*

Text	Extratextual Conversation
(pp. 1–9)	
If you give a pig a pancake	Adult: *Pan* and *cake* are two little words.
She'll want some syrup to go with it.	What happens when we squeeze them together? *Pancake*! Yum. I love pancakes!

45

You'll give her some of your favorite maple syrup.	Adult: *Maple* is a big word. It also has two parts. We can clap for the parts of *maple* [points to word]. *Ma-* [clap] *-ple* [clap].
She'll probably get all sticky.	Adult: *Sticky* is a big word, too. It has two parts. Can you clap for all of the parts in *sticky*?
So she'll want to take a bath.	Adult: *B-ath*. What word would we get if we put those sounds together?
She'll ask you for some bubbles.	Adult: *Bubbles* is a big word that has two parts. Let me clap it out for you: *Bu-* [clap] *-bbles* [clap]. Can you try it with me? *Bu-* [clap] *-bbles* [clap].
When you give her the bubbles, she'll probably ask you for a toy. You'll have to find your rubber duck.	Adult: There's that word *bubbles* again. Remember that the word *bubbles* has two parts. Can you try to clap it out by yourself?
The duck will remind her of the farm where she was born. She might feel homesick and want to visit her family.	Adult: *Homesick* is another big word. Let's say *homesick* without the *home.*

For this activity, adults can make the task more challenging as children gain competence in segmenting and blending. It is easiest to have children begin by manipulating compound words, where the syllables are also words themselves (e.g., *homesick*). However, it is also possible to break down a word into its onset and rime unit (e.g., /b/-/ath/), or its individual phonemes (b-a-th) to make the activity more challenging.

What Rhymes With That?

Objective: To demonstrate rhyme awareness and rhyme production

Storybook: *In the Tall, Tall Grass* (1991) by Denise Fleming

Description: This brightly colored book about creatures that live in the tall, tall grass provides many opportunities for children to become aware of and produce rhyme. On each page, there are a few boldly printed words, including multiple words that rhyme.

In the Tall, Tall Grass provides many examples of words that rhyme. It is a good book for helping children to develop an awareness of rhyme and to try to produce new rhymes themselves. To foster an interest in rhyming words, adults are encouraged to use the following two techniques throughout the reading:

1. To comment on how the words in the story rhyme

2. To ask children to think of words that rhyme with simple words in the book

Interactive Reading Experience Using *In the Tall, Tall Grass*

Text	Extratextual Conversation
(pp. 1–10)	
In the tall, tall grass...	Adult: The word *tall* is on this page twice [points to each word]. Can you think of any words that might rhyme with *tall*?
Crunch, munch, caterpillars lunch	Adult: There are three words on this page that rhyme! Look here: *crunch*, *munch*, and *lunch* [points to each word].
Dart, dip, hummingbirds sip	Adult: *Dip* and *sip* rhyme on this page [points to each word]. Can you think of another word that would rhyme with *dip* and *sip*?
Strum, drum, bees hum	Adult: Wow! There are a lot of rhymes in this book. Can you tell me what words rhyme on this page?
Crack, snap, wings flap	Adult: *Snap* and *flap* rhyme, too! Let me think of some other words that might rhyme with them. I think *cap* and *lap* would rhyme with *snap* and *flap*.

For this activity, adults should note that recognizing words that rhyme is easier for children than producing the rhymes themselves.

Start at the Beginning

Objective: To demonstrate awareness of and produce beginning sounds

Storybook: *Sheep in a Shop* (1991) by Nancy Shaw, illustrated by Margot Apple

Description: There's a birthday, and the sheep must find a present for the party! This book includes many examples of beginning sounds, and it also includes many instances of rhyme.

Sheep in a Shop provides many examples of words that have the same first sound. It also includes many words that rhyme, so adults can use this book to reinforce the lessons learned in Activity 4.3. For this storybook, adults are encouraged to use the following three techniques throughout the reading:

1. To comment on the beginning sounds of words

2. To ask children to make the first sounds of words themselves

3. To ask children to say a word as slowly as they can to help them to isolate the first sound in the word

Interactive Reading Experience Using *Sheep in a Shop*

Text	Extratextual Conversation
(pp. 1–6)	
A birthday's coming. Hip Hooray!	Adult: The sheep must be excited about their birthday party. I see something else exciting—two words that start with the same exact sound! *Hip* and *Hooray* both start with the same sound [points to words]: *Hhhh.*
Five sheep shop for the big, big day.	Adult: I see two more words that start with the same sound: *Sh-sh-sheep* and *sh-sh-shop.* What sound do both words start with? I want you to say *sheep* as slowly as you can. Ready. Go ahead.
	Child: Shhhh.
	Adult: OK, stop. That's the first sound in sheep. Try it again.
	Child: Shhh...sheep and shop.
	Adult: Good job!
Sheep find rackets. Sheep find rockets.	Adult: *Rackets* and *rockets* both start with the same sound, too. *Rrrrr.* Will you make that sound with me?
	Adult and child: *Rrrrr.*

	Adult: Wow! That was great! *Rrrrrrackets* and *Rrrrrrockets*.
Sheep find jackets full of pockets.	Adult: I see two more words that start with the same sound: *Find* and *full* [points to the words]. Can you tell me what sound they both start with?
Sheep find blocks. Sheep wind clocks.	Adult: There's that word *sheep* again. Can you remember the sound that *sheep* starts with?

Note that it is easier for a child to learn about beginning sounds than ending sounds. It is also easier for children to attend to beginning sounds and ending sounds when they are *singletons* (just one phoneme alone, like the beginning sound /s/ in *sun* and *sock*) rather than *consonant clusters* (combinations of phonemes, like the beginning sound /st/ in *star* and *story*). The easier the word structure, the easier it is for children to focus on the phonological units; by contrast, the more complex the word structure, the more scaffolding will be required by the adult to assist the child's performance.

Ending on a Same Note

Objective: To demonstrate awareness of and produce final sounds

Storybook: *The Big Hat* (1999) by Bobby Lynn Maslen

Description: This book is part of a series called *Bob Books Fun!* and is a short story that uses very simple words. Many of the words in this series of books end with the same sound, so this is a great book for children to begin to learn about final sounds.

The Big Hat provides a number of words that have the same final sound that children can listen for. Because pointing out the final sounds of words is the most difficult activity for children in this chapter, we selected a simpler book in order to make the task easier for children. Adults are asked to use the following techniques when discussing final sounds with a child:

1. To comment on the final sounds of words
2. To ask children to attend to final sounds within the book

Interactive Reading Experience Using *The Big Hat*

Text (pp. 1–8)	Extratextual Conversation
Rex was a big dog.	Adult: *Big* and *dog* both end with the same sound [points to words and

49

	emphasizes final sound]. /g/ Can you say that with me?
	Adult and child: /g/
Rex sat on the hat.	Adult: There are two words that end with the same sound in this sentence. Do you know what they are?
Max was mad at Rex.	Adult: Wow! This sentence has two words that end with the same sound, too. *Max* and *Rex* [emphasizes final ending of words].
Tex was mad at Rex.	Adult: Listen carefully. Can you tell me which two words end with the same sound? Here's a hint: It's the same final sound that we just heard on the last page.

Additional Storybooks for Building Phonological Awareness

Bear Snores On (2001) by Karma Wilson, illustrated by Jane Chapman

This story is about a bear that slumbers through a cold winter while other animals throw a party in his cave. This story features many sentences of varying lengths, and it also includes several instances of beginning sounds and rhyme, making it a wonderful book to practice many of the activities featured in this chapter.

Chicka Chicka Boom Boom (1989) by Bill Martin Jr and John Archambault, illustrated by Lois Ehlert

This is a fun alphabet book that provides children with a number of opportunities to practice rhyming concepts. This book includes a lot of repetition, so it may be ideal for those children who are just learning how to rhyme.

Froggy Gets Dressed (1992) by Jonathan London, illustrated by Frank Remkiewicz

In this story, Froggy wants to go out and play in the snow even though he is supposed to be sleeping all winter. This story provides some wonderful examples of beginning sounds (e.g., *Zup! Zat! Zwit!*) and also includes compound words (e.g., *outside, underwear*) that are easier for children to segment.

Goose on the Loose (2001) by Phil Roxbee Cox, illustrated by Stephen Cartwright

This lift-the-flap book about a goose who is riding around town on her scooter provides many instances of rhyme. It also provides many places for adults to comment on beginning sounds (e.g., *Rooster Ron*).

In the Small, Small Pond (1993) by Denise Fleming

Similar in nature to *In the Tall, Tall Grass*, this boldly colored book tells a tale of creatures who live in a pond. This book contains many opportunities for children to produce and become aware of rhyme. There are also a number of words in the story that would facilitate a lesson on beginning sounds (e.g., *waddle, wade*).

Sam Sheep Can't Sleep (2000) by Phil Roxbee Cox, illustrated by Stephen Cartwright

This adventure about a sheep that cannot sleep provides many opportunities for children to become aware of rhyme. The sentences and words in this story are simple, which may make it easier for children to understand. This story can also be used to teach the concept of segmenting sentences. However, because most words have only one syllable, this story may not be ideal for teaching children how to segment and blend words.

Sheep Out to Eat (1992) by Nancy Shaw, illustrated by Margot Apple

This story details the adventures of sheep as they try to eat out at a restaurant. This book includes many instances of rhyme and provides opportunities for children to discuss beginning sounds.

There Was an Old Lady Who Swallowed a Fly (1997) by Simms Taback

This folk tale about an old woman who swallows a fly (and then swallows a spider to eat the fly) does not end well for the old woman. However, it does provide many good opportunities for children to become aware of and produce rhyme. It also provides many opportunities to discuss print concepts.

Where's Curly? (2003) by Heather Amery, illustrated by Stephen Cartwright

This lift-the-flap book follows Poppy and Sam as they look for Curly the Pig. It contains many words that are appropriate for segmentation activities, such as *farmyard, everywhere,* and *woodshed*.

Zin! Zin! Zin! A Violin (1995) by Lloyd Moss, illustrated by Marjorie Priceman

This entertaining story about the instruments that make up an orchestra is brightly illustrated and includes many opportunities for learning about rhyme. With many phrases such as "mournful moan," it also provides examples for children to think about beginning sounds. This story is somewhat complex for preschoolers and includes many novel words, such as *nonet*.

This chapter has identified specific approaches to supporting phonological knowledge in young children within the shared storybook reading interaction. Phonological knowledge, also termed phonological awareness, is an important achievement during early childhood, and skills in this area help to ease children's transition to learning to read. Helping children develop their sensitivities to words, syllables, and individual sounds as units of spoken language can be readily integrated into shared reading interactions. Adults can scaffold children's awareness of these sound units by helping with difficult tasks and relinquishing this help as children progress. Chapter 5 discusses an area of early literacy development that, like phonological knowledge, helps prepare children for learning how to read. This area of development, alphabet knowledge, describes children's knowledge of the individual letters of the alphabet. Along with phonological knowledge, alphabet knowledge helps children crack the code of how letters and sounds go together in the written alphabetic language.

CHAPTER 5

Building Alphabet Knowledge: Learning About the Features and Names of Letters

Alphabet knowledge has received considerable attention as an important aspect of literacy development during the preschool and kindergarten years. Children who come to beginning reading instruction with well-developed knowledge of the alphabet progress more readily in that instruction compared to children who do not have this knowledge (e.g., Walpole, Chow, & Justice, 2004), and preschoolers' knowledge of the alphabet is one of the better predictors of reading success (Storch & Whitehurst, 2002). Put simply, *alphabet knowledge* describes children's knowledge about the letters of the alphabet. However, this definition should not be interpreted into an educational practice whereby we drill young children to memorize all the letters. Research suggests that children who have well-developed knowledge of the alphabet have had more experiences with the alphabet across diverse types of literacy genres (Senechal, LeFevre, Thomas, & Daley, 1998). The research of Senechal and colleagues has suggested that the amount of experience children have with books in the home environment is one of the better predictors of alphabet knowledge in kindergarten and first grade. Experiences with the alphabet in meaningful and contextualized activities, such as interactive reading, can help children make connections between the alphabet letters and their broader purpose for reading. Therefore, as educators, we want to encourage children's early interest in the alphabet within the context of a large array of meaningful, contextualized, and engaging literacy activities. Interactive reading is an optimal way to foster children's emerging interest in letters as symbolic tools and to enhance children's early understanding of how letters work to carry meaning in written language.

How Alphabet Knowledge Develops

Children who are reared in literate households in which book reading experiences are frequent begin to show emerging knowledge of the alphabet during the first three years of life. Some children will even know a letter or two before their second birthday, particularly those children whose caregivers engage them often in playing with the alphabet (e.g., in books, with magnets). These children may, for instance, recognize some of the letters in their names, show interest in specific letters occurring in the environment on signs or labels, and may begin to write some letters with which they are especially familiar (Chaney, 1994). Children's knowledge of the alphabet is particularly evidenced in their gradual achievement in learning how to write their own names. Children move through a predictable sequence as they learn to write their own names, moving from a scribble to use of random symbols, to use of a few random symbols combined with a letter or two, to use of a majority of correct letters, to production of their names accurately (Welsch, Sullivan, & Justice, 2003). Many children reared in literate homes or who attend quality preschools move through these stages before their fifth birthday. By 5 years of age, children often are familiar with the letters that make up their own names, a phenomenon referred to as the "own-name advantage" (Treiman & Broderick, 1998). An informative study by Treiman and Broderick showed that 79% of preschoolers from middle class homes were able to identify the first letter in their own names, a figure that is particularly high compared to children reared in low-income homes (Justice & Ezell, 2001). For the latter group, less than 50% of preschoolers could name the first letter of their own names. Also interesting is that children's acquisition of letter names appears to be related to the order of the alphabet (McBride-Chang, 1999), which is likely due to children's greater amount of exposure to the beginning letters of the alphabet.

An important concept for educators and parents to understand is that the development of alphabet knowledge is a cultural phenomenon rather than a developmental phenomenon. Children's learning about the alphabet is driven by their cultural and social experiences with the world around them more so than any sort of developmental force. This is presumably why children with few experiences with print and books in the home environment have underdeveloped knowledge about the alphabet compared to children with more experiences with print (e.g., Bowey, 1995; Fernandez-Fein & Baker, 1997). When considering how to educate children about the alphabet, educators and parents should keep in mind these most important rules of thumb—to indoctrinate children to viewing the alphabet as an object worthy of interest and attention as early as possible and to understand that the concept of "developmental appropriateness" should not hold back these experiences. A 1-year-old child being reared with exposure to an alphabetic system is able to consider aspects of the alphabet as interesting as any other symbol system, including spoken words, stuffed animals, and storybooks.

Early indoctrination into how the alphabet works is important in a society that expects children, by age 5, to be relatively knowledgeable about the alphabet as a written language system. Kindergarten programs increasingly emphasize children s learning of the correspondence between letters (graphemes) and sounds (phonemes) and children's application of this knowledge to beginning reading. Instruction that focuses on helping children discover the systematic relationships between letters and sounds, or *phonics*, is most useful for children who are familiar with the alphabet. Put another way, children who come to kindergarten with sophisticated knowledge of the letters are better able to profit from phonics instruction and leave kindergarten better prepared for first-grade reading instruction. In turn, these children tend to learn to read more quickly than children who enter kindergarten with only limited knowledge of the alphabet (Walpole et al., 2004). Helping parents to support their children's alphabet knowledge in the home environment is an important goal of early education. Below, we provide some tips for parents to develop children's alphabet knowledge in the home environment.

ALPHabet KnoWLeDGe TiPS for parents

Parents can help foster an understanding of alphabet knowledge in their children in many ways. One fun way to help children learn about letters is to create characters for each of the letters, draw them, and have children color them in and talk about them. Here are some examples:

- Turn a lowercase letter *b* into a bumblebee by adding wings, stripes, and a stinger.

- Turn the letter *Z* into a zebra by adding a head, tail, and some stripes. Your role is primarily to show your child that the alphabet is interesting and worthy of attention. Children who consider the alphabet interesting will learn more about the alphabet on their own as they seek it out and attend to it in their environments. If your child comes to view the letter *Z* as interesting because of her play at home with a parent, she will probably start to see the *Z* in everything (in the branches of a tree, on a sign, in a book) and point it out to others around her.

- Make an alphabet book with different animals representing each letter.

How Interactive Reading Supports
the Development of Alphabet Knowledge

The first few years of life provide an important foundation for establishing children's familiarity with the alphabet. This learning should be fun and adventuresome for young children; a central premise of this chapter is that inciting early interest in print can promote children's long-term interest in reading and literacy. Many children enjoy the symbolic nature of oral language, which provides them a means to share their needs, interests, and experiences with others through their words. Likewise, children can be guided early in life to appreciate the symbolic nature of written language, which unlocks for them an additional tool for expressing themselves to others. The role of the early educator—including teachers, parents, and other specialists—is to promote children's familiarity and interest in the alphabet in a variety of contexts. Storybook reading provides a highly contextualized and engaging springboard for fostering children's initial discoveries about the alphabet, influencing both familiarity and interest. In fact, in our opinion, books provide an avenue for alphabetic discoveries that is surpassed by no other early childhood activity. Research by Justice and Ezell (2002) supports the point of using books to enhance children's familiarity with the alphabet. Justice and Ezell measured the knowledge of individual letters of the alphabet of 30 children attending a Head Start program at the start and end of a two-month period. Half the children participated in regular storybook reading sessions (24 sessions in two months) that included discussion about the pictures in the books, whereas the other half participated in regular sessions that included discussion about letters and words in the books. Children who participated in the picture-focused reading sessions learned, on average, only one additional alphabet letter over the two-month period. By contrast, children who participated in the print-focused reading sessions learned an average of four additional letters during the two months. This suggests that storybook reading interactions that feature conversation about the pictures do not stimulate alphabet learning a great deal but that including a more explicit focus on the alphabet can increase alphabet learning by about fourfold. The intentional educator can capitalize on these research discoveries to rouse a child's long-term interest in the alphabetic code and knowledge about the individual letters.

Interactive Reading Activities for Building
Alphabet Knowledge

Here we present titles and descriptions of storybooks that provide an excellent context for developing children's early familiarity and interest in alphabet knowledge. We also provide guidance for specific interactional approaches adult readers can use to guide children's development of alphabetic skills. These activities are arranged to enable children to achieve the following objectives:

1. To develop an interest in alphabet letters
2. To recognize that letters are a specific type of print unit
3. To recognize the differences between letters
4. To identify several letters in their own names
5. To identify several additional letters

These objectives are certainly not all the possible objectives that can be addressed in the area of alphabet knowledge during interactive reading. However, by developing a foundational level of skill in these areas, the child is likely to have the precursory knowledge and interest concerning the alphabet to propel further discoveries within interactive reading as well as other diverse literacy contexts.

Letters on the Bus

Objective: To develop an interest in alphabet letters

Storybook: *School Bus* (1984) by Donald Crews

Description: This richly illustrated storybook features print-salient qualities: few words per page, repetitive print, and print embedded in the illustrations, many of which are familiar terms for children (e.g., *stop, bus, walk*). This storybook can foster highly contextualized adult–child interactions about print in general and alphabet letters specifically.

School Bus is a useful storybook to encourage a child's interest in alphabet letters, as are other storybooks by Donald Crews (e.g., *Flying*, 1986; *Harbor*, 1982; *Sail Away*, 1995). Throughout this book, letters are a prominent feature within both the text and the illustrations. To encourage an interest in the alphabet, the adult is encouraged to use the following two techniques throughout the reading:

1. Comment on letters
2. Point to specific letters

In using these techniques, the goal is not to engage the child in conversations about letters but to incite an interest in the alphabet as an important and relevant part of the storybook reading experience. The adult does this by simply commenting about letters without questioning—unlike questioning, adult commenting does not obligate the child to respond. Commenting, coupled with pointing, guides the child's visual attention toward the alphabet as a prominent and interesting part of the storybook, as demonstrated in the following example.

Interactive Reading Experience Using *School Bus*

Text	Extratextual Conversation
(pp. 1–10)	
Yellow school bus.	Adult: Wow! There are a lot of buses. And on each bus it says, *School Bus* [points to the two words]. *School Bus* starts with an *S* and ends with an *S* [points to each letter].
Large and small.	Adult: And there it says *School Bus* again on top of the little bus [points to the two words]. And there's an *S* and an *S* [points to each letter]. We saw those letters on the last page.
Empty yellow buses cross the town.	Adult: There's an *S* again—right on the back of that bus [points to the letter *S*]. Lots of *S*s in this book.
STOP.	Adult: There's an *S* in this word, right there [points to the letter *S*].
GO.	Adult: No *S* in that word—there's a *G* and an *O* [points to the letters *G* and *O*].

Again, what is important to note in the preceding extratextual conversation is that there is no obligation for the child to participate in the alphabet-focused commentary. Instead, the adult is taking the lead in showing the child that the alphabet—specifically the letter *S*—is an object that is worthy of attention. The adult does not require that the child discuss the letter but focuses on facilitating the child's interest in and attention to the alphabet within the context of an enjoyable reading session. Children can chime in and engage in alphabet-focused conversation if they are so enticed, but this level of participation is clearly not required.

ACTIVITY 5.2

Letters on the Ground

Objective: To recognize that letters are a specific type of print unit

Storybook: *The Awful Aardvarks Go to School* (1997) by Reeve Lindbergh, illustrated by Tracey Campbell Pearson

Description: This rhyming storybook provides an abundance of opportunities for adults and children to talk about the alphabet letters. This fun book tells the story of a family of aardvarks who go to school and cause lots of trouble. The narrative features a rhyming pattern that emphasizes alliteration and rhyming patterns that flow from *A* to *Z* (e.g., "They angered the Anteater, Ate All the Ants, and Bullied the Bunny, they pulled down his pants!"). In addition to provoking fun conversation about the aardvarks' antics, the storybook provides an outstanding springboard for talking about letters and sounds. This is bolstered by the authors' inventive inclusion of the entire alphabet string printed across the top of each page.

To encourage children's awareness of alphabet letters as specific types of print units, the adult can comment about the alphabet within the context of the storybook reading. The adult can focus this commentary on explaining how letters work in storybooks and how letters are different than other types of print (e.g., numbers, words, punctuation units). Using the storybook, the adult can point out how uppercase letters are different than lowercase letters, a concept that is supported by the inclusion of uppercase and lowercase letters presented along the top of each page. In using these techniques, the goal is to *expose* children to key concepts about the alphabet letters. For young children, mastery is not expected, yet the adult leads the child's learning to target concepts that are beyond the child's independent skills though not so difficult as to frustrate the child.

Interactive Reading Experience Using *The Awful Aardvarks Go to School*

Text	Extratextual Conversation
(title page and pp. 1–2)	
The Awful Aardvarks Go to School	Adult: That's the name of this book. Look at all those letters lying on the ground. I wonder if the chicken is going to eat them! I hope not.
	Child: He will get sick!
	Adult: You're right. We really shouldn't eat letters. You know that letter. It's an *A*. That is an uppercase *A*, and that is a lowercase *a*.
	Child: Uppercase *A*, lowercase *a*.
	Adult: You got it.
The day the Aardvarks came into our school was Alphabet Awful—they broke every rule!	Adult: Uh oh. The aardvarks break some rules What are some rules you think the aardvarks are going to break?

Child: Throwing stuff.

Adult: Yes, you see paper airplanes flying here. No throwing in the classroom is a good rule.

Adult: Look at all these letters up here at the top. Do you want to say them with me?

Child: *A, B, C...Z.*

Adult: That's great! See, these letters go into these words.

Child: Those are the words.

Adult: Right, and these letters make the words. See, this *s* goes into this word, *school.*

Child: *S* in school. And that *T* goes in this word.

Adult: Yes. That word has a *T.* That is great. You put the letter into the word! It says, "The."

Note how the adult uses a variety of techniques to draw the child's attention to the letters and to think about how letters and words are different types of print units. The adult uses the storybook as a springboard for these alphabet-focused conversations, *contextualizing* a conversation focused on abstract concepts by placing it within the familiar context of an interesting and meaningful storybook. Repeated exposure to such concepts will gradually shape the child's understanding of letters as print units.

ACTIVITY 5.3

The Old Man's Alphabet

Objective: To recognize the differences between letters

Storybook: *This Old Man* (2000), illustrated by Carol Jones

Description: This richly illustrated rhyming book shares the "This Old Man" poem with which most adults are familiar: "This old man he played...ONE. He played nick nack on my...." Children find great delight in watching what the old man strikes with a set of drumsticks, and with time they become very familiar with the poem and song that go with it. This book also has a useful feature for promoting children's interest in alphabet letters and discussing the distinctive features of letters: on each page, the all-capital-letter printing of the numbers (e.g., *he played...ONE*) and the words that rhyme with these numbers (*...DRUM*). Because the storybook does not present a traditional narrative story, stopping to talk about letters and words does not detract greatly from the text.

When reading *This Old Man*, adults can use the storybook as a springboard to introduce conversation focused on the alphabet letters, particularly the distinctive features of various letters. The storybook facilitates this kind of conversation by presenting words throughout the book in uppercase letters, such as *ONE, TWO, THREE* and *DRUM, SHOE,* and *KNEE.* Children become knowledgeable about the rhyming patterns in the book relatively quickly, which allows them to focus their resources and interests on other features of the book without being distracted. These words can be used as opportunities to talk about how each letter has its own special features and name, as demonstrated in the following example of an adult–child shared reading experience using *This Old Man.*

Interactive Reading Experience Using *This Old Man*

Text	Extratextual Conversation
(pp. 1–7)	
This old man he played... ONE. He played nick nack on my...	Adult: What do you think he'll play nick nack on?
	Child: Drum!
	Adult: Oh, you remember from last time! You are right: It's nick nack on my drum. Here it says *drum.*
	Child: Drum.
	Adult: *D-R-U-M.* Which one is the *M*; can you find it?
	Child: This one? [points to *D*]
	Adult: That's a *D*. See, it has a big belly that hangs out on its side [traces *D* with finger]. This one is the *M*. Like mountains. Played nick nack on my drum. Pretty silly.
This old man he played... TWO. He played nick nack on my...	Child: Shoe.
	Adult: You got it. You knew it before I did.
	Child: I knew it. That says *shoe.*
	Adult: Right on. *S-H-O-E.* Look at how the *O* is like a big circle.
	Child: It's a big circle [traces the *O* with his finger].

Adult: But the *S* is like a snake. It is different than the *O*. Move your finger like this [moves finger along the *S*].

Child: *S.*

Adult: Right. These are all different letters. *S-H-O-E.*

One can see how the storybook and its salient print features provide a ready context for a metalinguistic conversation focused on the distinctive features of different letters. With repeated engagement in conversations like the one in this activity, the child learns that the alphabet is an object worthy of conversation and simultaneously develops a familiarity with the unique visual representation of each letter.

The Alphabet Cat

Objective: To identify several letters in his or her own name

Storybook: *Top Cat* (1998) by Lois Ehlert

Description: This book is engaging, with its unique story line, creative illustrations, and innovative print features on all book pages—all common features of Ehlert's children's books. In this book, a new cat is brought into a home and the veteran cat feels threatened. Soon, however, the two cats become friends and cause loads of trouble. Ehlert uses very few words to tell her story, and these words are in large print, making them easy to talk about and focus upon in alphabet-centered discussions. Also, as in other Ehlert books, she has small printed words sprinkled across the page, such as the words "swish swish" next to a cat's tail and the "jingle jingle" next to the bell on a cat's collar. These added print features provide excellent conversation starters to talk to children about print, including the alphabet.

Egocentric thinking is a unique mark of childhood that adults can cultivate when developing children's knowledge of the alphabet. Often, the earliest letters learned by children are the letters of their own names, with knowledge of their first initial developing first. Children who know just a few letters of the alphabet tend to know their own first initial and the first initial of names of a few family members, such as a brother and sister. Using storybooks to foster children's knowledge of the letters in their own names and the names of others close to them is a useful technique for building children's alphabet knowledge. Adults should not hold back from incorporating print-focused conversations into storybook reading experiences, as demonstrated in the following example.

Interactive Reading Experience Using *Top Cat*

Text	Extratextual Conversation
(pp. 9–12)	

And I don't like your cute little face.

Adult: Oh, that's not very nice!

Child: He is naughty.

Adult: That cat is being very naughty. I think he has a cute face.

Look at these words here. See this first big letter? Do you know this one?

Child: *A!*

Adult: Yes, *A* like in your name.

Child: *A* for Alexis.

Adult: *A* for Alexis. And this one is a...

Child: I don't know.

Adult: This is the letter *I*. Like in Isaac. You know Isaac.

Child: Yes, he's in my class.

Adult: *I* for Isaac. What other letters are in your name? Let's see if we can find some. Let's look for an *L*.

Child: I don't know what it looks like.

Adult: Well, this is a lowercase *l* here. This one. That's the *l* that is in your name. Let's keep looking for *L*s while we read this.

I'll fight you and bite you behind the ear...

Child: I see one!

Adult: What do you see?

Child: *L*s. *L, L.*

Adult: Look at that. Two *l*s in the word *I'll*. You found two *l*s. Like in your name. I'm impressed.

In this storybook reading activity using Ehlert's *Top Cat*, the large narrative print provides both the adult and the child the opportunity to talk about letters, particularly those letters in the child's name. When children read books with adults, they tend to follow the lead of the adult in discovering salient aspects of the book. If adults talk about the pictures, children will do so also. If adults talk about print, including letters of the alphabet, children will do that also (Justice, Weber, Ezell, & Bakeman, 2002). Here, the adult shows the child that storybooks provide an appropriate context for talking about letters, and the child readily begins to explore on her own the extent to which books feature the letters of her name.

Door Starts With D

Objective: To identify several additional letters

Storybook: *Nibbly Mouse* (1994) by David Drew, illustrated by Penny Newman

Description: This creative picture book sets children on a mission to discover what Nibbly Mouse finds upon eating holes in various things. For instance, Nibbly Mouse eats a hole in a cake...can you imagine what she saw? Children get two types of clues to guess what Nibbly Mouse finds. The first clue is a hole in the page that reveals a small piece of the next illustration. The second clue is a letter—for instance, "it starts with a *d*." Nibbly Mouse sees things in this book that start with a *d* (*door*), a *b* (*blanket*), and a *c* (*cake*), among others. The book provides a ready context for engaging children in stimulating guessing games, with a built-in mechanism for incorporating the alphabet into these games.

Once children realize that the alphabet is a worthy object of their attention and they have come to identify a few letters—particularly those in their own names—adults must provide them with additional learning opportunities to become familiar with all the other letters. This familiarity will not happen in a day; instead, children need multiple exposures to the 26 letters in a variety of contexts and with different levels of support. For each letter, children will also need to learn both the uppercase and lowercase forms. Books like *Nibbly Mouse* provide excellent targeted opportunities to engage children in focused conversations about specific letters; in *Nibbly Mouse*, attention focuses on the lowercase letters *b*, *t*, *c*, and *d* as children play guessing games to figure out what Nibbly Mouse sees. The context of this book provides a natural scaffold for enticing children to study different letters and to think about how they sound and what they do.

Interactive Reading Experience Using *Nibbly Mouse*

Text	Extratextual Conversation
(pp. 8–11)	
Nibbly Mouse ate a hole in my basket.	Adult: Oh, it starts with *c*.
Now what can this be? It starts with c.	Child: What starts with *c*?

Adult: Well, that's your job. This is the letter *c*, and we have to think of things that start with a *c*.

Child: That's a *c*.

Adult: Yes. This is a *c*. It's a letter. It makes the /k/ sound. And it's a clue for us about what Nibbly Mouse sees. Let's see. Some things that start with the letter *c...Camera. Cookie. Cat.* What do you think?

Child: *Cat.*

Adult: *Cat* starts with *c*. Good. Let's see.

Child: *Cake*!

Adult: Ahh, he found *cake. Cake* does start with *c*. We didn't think of that.

Child: I thought of it.

Adult: Oh, you did! Let's do another one.

Then what did she see? It starts with d.   Child: Starts with *d*.

Adult: Good! That's a *d* there. It makes the sound /d/.

Child: *d*.

Adult: Starts with *d*.

Child: *Candle.*

Adult: That's a candle on the cake. But we need to think of things that start with the letter *d*. *d* makes a /d/ sound. *Dog, dandelion, daisy*...The letter *d*. Hmmm.

Child: *Windows*!

Adult: Those do look like windows through the hole. But *window*, /w/, doesn't start with *d*. It starts with *w*. Let's take a look.

Child: *Door.*

Adult: *Door* starts with *d*. That's the *d*.

In the preceding extratextual conversation, the child is unfamiliar with the letters being discussed but, under the guidance of a supportive educator, is also willing to focus on the letters and think about how they work. The adult uses this storybook to build the child's familiarity with new letters. With repeated exposures in the context of this book and other learning opportunities, the child will become very familiar with the letters *c* and *d* and will likely soon generate the sounds that go with these letters as well as words that start with the letters. This well-crafted storybook helps children make connections between letters, sounds, and the meaning that both represent. The adult uses the storybook to support children's discoveries as they move from novices to experts.

Additional Storybooks for Building Alphabet Knowledge

David Gets in Trouble (2002) by David Shannon

This simple yet enjoyable storybook has David describing all the excuses he uses when he gets in trouble. These include "I couldn't help it," "I forgot," and the ubiquitous "The dog ate my homework." Children have an enjoyable time commiserating with David's failures (and excuses). What is also unusual about this book is that the narrative print appears crafted by a child's hand and contains very few words per page. One page, for instance, has just these words: "I forgot!" While discussing David and his many excuses, adults can also use this book to begin to develop children's awareness of different letters and how they are used to create meaning.

Dear Mrs. LaRue: Letters From Obedience School (2002) by Mark Teague

Ike the dog writes letters to his owner as he thinks about escaping from his strict obedience school. This book features many instances of print embedded in pictures. Adults can use this embedded print as a means to comment on the alphabet letters and the meaning that they carry.

Dear Zoo (1982) by Rod Campbell

This lift-the-flap book has a predictable yet enjoyable sequence of events as animals are sent one by one from the zoo and then rejected for various reasons (e.g., the camel is sent back because he is too grumpy). The predictability of the text, in addition to its large print and few words per page, provides an easy venue for engaging children in talk about letters and print.

Freight Train (1978) by Donald Crews

Like all of Crews's excellent books for young children, *Freight Train* provides a simple story supported by colorful and rich illustrations. The simple text speaks to the interest in trains common to nearly all children, and in this book a train is explored as it moves over a bridge and through a tunnel to finally disappear. Few words occur on each page, and these appear in different colors, which entice children's interest. The adult can help children to focus on the words ("Look, these words are purple!") and use the words to initiate talk about the different attributes of letters and to search for letters familiar to the child.

Froggy Plays Soccer (1999) by Jonathan London, illustrated by Frank Remkiewicz

This book tells the story of a frog and his soccer team as they learn some important rules about how to handle a soccer ball, namely how to "head it, boot it, knee it, and shoot it" without using their hands. *Froggy Plays Soccer* features patterns of repeated letters. For example, on pages 2 and 3, the letter *z* is used seven times, making this book a good choice for commenting on alphabet letters that children may see less frequently.

Hug (2000) by Jez Alborough

This book is sure to be loved by infants and grandparents alike, with its focus on the importance of relationships and—yes—hugs. In this picture book, which features very few words, Bobo the monkey walks through the forest and becomes saddened at the many hugs he witnesses among animals (e.g., snakes hugging, hippos hugging). He repeats the word *hug* over and over on each page, yelling it with glee when he finds his mother at the end and they unite in a warm embrace. Because *Hug* features so few words and the same word over and over in all-capital letters, children and adults can talk about these letters and incorporate an alphabet-focused conversation within a broader discussion of the relationship between parents and children.

Maisy at the Fair (2001) by Lucy Cousins

In this brightly illustrated book, Maisy and friends spend the day riding rides, eating, and taking in all of the sights at the fair. This book highlights print by placing all text on the left-hand pages and all pictures on the right-hand pages, making it appropriate for focusing on specific words and letters apart from the story.

Rumble in the Jungle (1997) by Giles Andreae, illustrated by David Wojtowycz

This book features informative rhyming verses about several jungle animals. It is particularly useful for incorporating discussion of alphabet letters because outside of the text, each animal name is featured in large print, along with a sound that animal might make.

Spot's First Walk (1981) **by Eric Hill**

In this book, Spot takes a walk and sees many interesting things. The appeal of Spot books to young children is well known by most adults—children like the simple story line and always enjoy lifting the flaps, which allows them to participate in the story. The Spot books provide an additional valuable feature that may be less obvious, and that is the minimalist use of print—few words per page and a large font. In this book, as Spot takes his walk, adults can use the large print to their advantage to engage children in discussions about different letters, such as the *S* that occurs every time Spot's name appears.

26 Letters and 99 Cents (1987) **by Tana Hoban**

This book contains the 26 letters of the alphabet, in uppercase and lowercase, alongside pictures that start with each of the corresponding letter sounds. The letters are large and bright, each taking up one quarter of the page. The size and the presentation of uppercase and lowercase letters side by side make it easy for children to focus on specific features of the letters. At the end of the alphabet, the reader can flip the book upside down and count from 1 to 99 using pennies, nickels, dimes, and quarters.

This chapter has described interactive strategies that adults can use to foster children's knowledge of the alphabet during storybook reading. Specific objectives focused on helping children to develop an interest in alphabet letters, recognize that letters are a specific type of print unit, recognize the differences between letters, and identify several letters in their own names as well as additional letters. Adults can use shared storybook reading as an opportunity to build children's knowledge in all of these areas. Books particularly amenable to this type of learning are those featuring print as salient aspects of the book—that is, which include large, bold print and relatively few words per page. Some books provide multiple opportunities for talking about different letters and fostering children's interest in how the alphabet works. In chapter 6, strategies and storybooks for supporting children's narrative knowledge are described. Narrative knowledge refers to children's ability to produce and understand extended discourse describing real or fictional events. Like alphabet knowledge, the development of narrative skill can be readily supported in the interactive reading context.

Building Narrative Knowledge: Extending Language to Share Experiences and Ideas

*N*arrative knowledge describes a child's spoken and written descriptions of real or fictional events experienced in the past, the present, or the future. In a classic text on narrative, Labov (1972) defines a narrative to minimally contain two sequential independent clauses about the same past event. "Hey mom, guess what I made in art today?" is one way a preschooler might begin a narrative, followed by "We painted cats on the balloons." Over time, young children's narratives move from simple, chained sequences of events or ideas, which are not well organized or detailed, to more explicit and well-organized stories that follow a clear temporal or causal ordering of events.

Narratives are essentially *decontextualized monologues*. They are decontextualized in that rather than describing the here and now, their focus is often on people or characters not immediately present or on events removed from the current context. Narratives are considered monologues in the sense that they are largely uninterrupted streams of language, unlike conversations that are carried by two or more persons. In a conversation, an individual has the contextual support of the give-and-take of conversation. In a narrative, the individual is wholly responsible for the effectiveness of the communication.

How Narrative Knowledge Develops

Narrative development is an important element of early and later language development because narratives require children to utilize resources across all language domains in their production, to include syntax, morphology, semantics, phonology, and pragmatics. As children's language and literacy skills develop, their narratives become more sophisticated to contain more advanced syntax, greater coordination and cohesion across elements, more precise vocabulary, and a greater awareness of the informational needs of listeners. Although narrative skills begin to develop as early as age 2, children generally are not able to construct true narratives with a problem and resolution (or high point) until around age 4 (Kaderavek & Sulzby, 2000; Peterson, 1990). Two-year-olds, for instance, might try to describe an event for a listener without providing a clear introduction, middle, or end to the story. Children's early narratives may include only a minimal description of the participants, time, and location relevant to the event and may contain only a series of events. For instance, a 3-year-old's narrative might look like this:

He in the water. Running. Splashing. Getting out. The end.

Adelaide, the 2-year-old daughter of one of the authors, has one standard fictional narrative that she is able to produce when prompted, which goes like this:

Mother:	Tell me a story.
Adelaide:	Once upon a time.
Mother:	Is there more?
Adelaide:	There was a girl.
Mother:	Anything else?
Adelaide:	There was a person.
Mother:	And?
Adelaide:	The end.

As can be seen in this example—typical for a 2- or 3-year-old—children's earliest narratives may fail to provide the listener with all information necessary for understanding the event. In some cases, essential information may be omitted altogether. It is important to note that narratives become clearer for the listener as children's ability to consider the listener's perspective emerges (Peterson, 1990). Children's repertoire of linguistic devices, including adverbial time phrases (e.g., *yesterday, this morning*), verb morphology (e.g., *had opened, will go*), and cohesive devices (e.g., *and, then, after that*) also grow from ages 3 to 5 years, thus increasing the comprehensibility and organization of their narratives.

Historically, persons interested in helping children develop their language skills often focused on discrete aspects of language, such as grammar, vocabulary, or phonology (e.g., see Hegde, 1985). Currently, most experts emphasize the importance of supporting language in children as an integrated whole and focusing on those elements of language that are most linked to academic and social success (Merritt, Culatta, & Trostle, 1998). The emphasis on narrative in this book as an important element of language to support in young children is based on this perspective. When comprehending and producing a narrative, whether it focuses on a real or imaginary event, the child must draw upon resources from all language domains. Thus, narrative is a complex, multidimensional language activity, and by helping the child to comprehend and produce narratives, the educator is building the child's language skills across multiple domains. Also, narrative skills are linked to both social and academic success, and they are necessary for sustaining conversations with peers and for following the content in academic texts and instructional lessons. Helping parents to support their children's narrative knowledge in the home environment is an important goal of early education, and below we provide some helpful tips for parents.

Narrative Knowledge Tips for Parents

We all know that using the telephone is a wonderful way to keep in touch with friends and relatives, but did you ever stop to consider how talking on the phone can be beneficial for children? When talking over the telephone, we lose many of the cues that support face-to-face conversation (e.g., facial expressions, gestures) and must use conversation that is more precise to carry our meaning. An interesting study suggests that talking on the telephone can boost children's narrative skills (Hutchison, 2001). Elementary school-age children who were part of a six-week language intervention that used telephone conversations included more utterances, words, and different words in their narratives than children who did not participate in the telephone intervention. Your child may also benefit from using the telephone. Here are some examples:

- Encourage your child to share news of his exciting soccer game or school field trip with relatives on the phone so that he can hone narrative skills while also building stronger emotional connections with loved ones.

- Allow your child to talk to friends on the phone and share stories. Children who participated in the telephone intervention (Hutchinson) included more advanced narrative characteristics in their stories, with more explicit descriptions, more clauses and phrases used to identify objects and locations, and greater elaboration of characters' emotional states.

How Interactive Reading Supports
the Development of Narrative Knowledge

Narrative skills are an important area of mastery for children from toddlerhood to the elementary years because they support the child's language skills across multiple domains. Additionally, the decontextualized language inherent in narratives supports the child's transition to the milieu of the classroom in which language is often removed from the present to focus on events from the past and the future (Peterson, Jesso, & McCabe, 1999). Narratives are also packed with what is known as *literate language*, which describes a specific type of language that is highly precise and is necessary when little context is available. To use literate language is to use language to render meaning without relying on contextual information. To compare language that requires contextual cues for its proper interpretation to literate language, consider the following hypothetical situation in which a 4-year-old and 16-year-old describe what happened last weekend:

4-year-old: And then we broke down. It was busted.

16-year-old: Our new car broke down on I-95 last weekend just past the outer loop of the beltway because the converter or something blew up.

It is the language of the 16-year-old that helps listeners create a much more accurate picture in their minds of what happened to the car last weekend. The difference between the two narratives is primarily that of literate language, with the adolescent using elaborated noun phrases (*our new car*), adverbial phrases (*last weekend*), conjunctions (*because*), and highly precise vocabulary (*beltway, converter*), all of which characterize literate language use (Curenton & Justice, 2004). Adults can foster children's narrative development and literate language use by exposing them to oral narratives as well as storybooks containing extended narratives that unfold over time or through causal sequences.

Interactive Reading Activities
for Building Narrative Knowledge

Here we present storybooks and interactional strategies designed to foster narrative knowledge. Activities are aligned to the following objectives that characterize important early achievements in narrative knowledge:

1. To discuss the sequence of events in a story

2. To discuss what happens to characters in a story

3. To discuss the location or setting of a story

4. To discuss reported speech used by characters in a story

5. To identify the high point of a story

Sequencing With Adverbs

Objective: To discuss the sequence of events in a story

Storybook: *The Very Hungry Caterpillar* (1994) by Eric Carle

Description: A tiny but hungry caterpillar travels during the week in search of food before he builds a cocoon and emerges as a beautiful butterfly. For each piece of food that the caterpillar eats through, he leaves a small hole that children can look through.

Adults can use interactive reading to expose children explicitly to the way in which story events unfold over time. In doing so, adverbs have an important place in specifying when and how events transpire. This activity includes a discussion of the sequence of events in a story, with a focus on adverbs. Adverbs allow elaboration on how and in what ways events occur as we tell narratives. They are an important aspect of literate language, in that they modify verbs and provide specification on time (e.g., *next*), manner (e.g., *quickly*), and degree (e.g., *hardly*).

In this activity, notice how the adult focuses upon the sequence of events in the story by using several adverbs. These types of words prompt children to *recall* events that have happened and *predict* what will happen next, both of which are important language functions for preschoolers. Notice also how the adult incorporates discussion of the days of the week in a natural way.

Interactive Reading Experience Using *The Very Hungry Caterpillar*

Text	Extratextual Conversation
(pp. 3–6)	
He started to look for some food.	Adult: What do you think the caterpillar will do *next*?
	Child: He's gonna eat an apple.
	Adult: I think you're right. I see an apple with a hole through it on the *next* page.

73

On Monday he ate through one apple. But he was still hungry.	Adult: Do you know what day comes before *Monday*?
	Child: *Sunday* comes before *Monday*.
	Adult: What day comes after *Monday*? Let's see if we can find out on the next page...*Tuesday*.
On Tuesday he ate through two pears, but he was still hungry.	Adult: Do you remember what the caterpillar ate *yesterday*?
	Child: Apples.
	Adult: Yes, *yesterday* was Monday and he ate an apple.
On Wednesday he ate through three plums, but he was still hungry.	Adult: How many pieces of fruit do you think the caterpillar will eat *tomorrow*?
	Child: I don't know.
	Adult: *First*, he ate one piece, *then* he ate two pieces, *next* he ate three pieces, so *tomorrow* he might eat four pieces of fruit.

Although the child who listens to *The Very Hungry Caterpillar* has ample opportunity to implicitly experience these adverbial concepts, the adult in this interaction shifts toward an explicit focus on these concepts to guide the child's learning. Language interventionists use the term *focused stimulation* to describe the adult's intentional use of repetitive input that helps children to induce the relationship between words, objects, and events (Girolametto et al., 1996). The adult provides heightened levels of input that are contingent on the child's object of attention. As shown in the preceding extratextual conversation, the adult is using focused stimulation to heighten the child's awareness of and exposure to adverbial concepts that help to sequence the story's events.

ACTIVITY 6.2

Awareness of Characters

Objective: To discuss what happens to characters in a story

Storybook: *Pete's a Pizza* (1998) by William Steig

Description: Pete is in a bad mood because it is raining outside and he can't go out to play. His mom and dad pretend to turn Pete into a pizza to cheer him up until the sun comes out. This book is a great choice for introducing children to characters because each of the three characters is physically distinct from the others and each contributes a different level of action to the story. Pete's dad acts as the main entertainer by creating the game and executing most of the pretend pizza-making actions; Pete's mom watches the interaction and occasionally lends support to Pete's father; and Pete, who is being entertained, is the recipient of a host of pretend pizza-making actions.

In this activity, we focus on characters and what happens to them in a story. This requires using action verbs (such as *chasing* and *fleeing*), mental verbs (such as *pondering* and *imagining*), and adverbs of time (such as *first* and *next*). *Pete's a Pizza* is a useful story for focusing on interactive discussions of characters and what happens to them. This story has only three main characters, with most of the action centered on a single main character, so children can easily distinguish between each of the participants. Children also have the opportunity to imagine that Pete is a pizza as they see Pete's mother and father treat him as if he were one of the ingredients.

Interactive Reading Experience Using *Pete's a Pizza*

Text	Extratextual Conversation
(pp. 7–10)	
Now the dough gets whirled and twirled up in the air.	Adult: Look, Pete's dad is tossing him in the air. Why is he doing that?
	Child: Because he's a pizza.
	Adult: Do you think Pete likes being tossed?
	Child: Yep, he's a pizza. He likes it.
Next, some oil is generously applied. (It's really water.)	Adult: Why does Pete's dad use water instead of real oil?
	Child: They're just pretending. He's not really a pizza.
Then comes some flour. (It's really talcum powder.)	Adult: How do you know they are pretending? Because they are using talcum powder. Talcum powder is for skin, not pizza!
And then some tomatoes. (They're really checkers.)	Adult: Look at Pete's mom. She's helping Pete's dad cover Pete with checkers. Why don't they use real tomatoes?
	Child: Because it's all pretend. That's so silly.

In this interactive reading experience, the adult primarily uses open-ended questions to entice the child to participate in the dialogue concerning the characters. Studies on the effects of interactive reading have shown that open-ended questions are an important ingredient for improving children's participation in interactive reading and in taking conversations to more abstract levels (e.g., Whitehurst et al., 1994). The adult uses a series of open-ended questions to guide the child's awareness of and interest in the characters. Notice too that the adult in the preceding extratextual conversation focuses upon the emotions that each of the characters in the book might be feeling at different points in the story.

Location, Location, Location

Objective: To discuss the location or setting of a story

Storybook: *Diary of a Worm* (2003) by Doreen Cronin, illustrated by Harry Bliss

Description: A worm chronicles his day-to-day adventures in a diary. Through the worm's diary, children learn about both the mishaps and joys experienced by school-age kids.

This activity focuses on the setting or settings in which a story occurs. Children often omit details regarding the setting in which events take place, even though an understanding of the setting is necessary for interpreting the meaning of events. Because the story of *Diary of a Worm* occurs across multiple settings, the book is ideal for guiding children to think about settings and to discuss them using literate language.

Interactive Reading Experience Using *Diary of a Worm*

Text (pp. 7–10)	Extratextual Conversation
April 4: Fishing season started today. We all dug deeper.	Adult: See the worms under the ground? They must be trying to hide from the fishermen who like to use them for bait. That is why it says, "We all dug deeper."
April 10: It rained all night and the ground was soaked. We spent the entire day on the sidewalk. Hopscotch is a very dangerous game.	Adult: They come out after the rain because they can move around without drying up when the ground is wet.
April 15: I forgot my lunch today. I got so hungry that I ate my homework.	Adult: Where does it look like these worms are? They're supposed to be at a school cafeteria.

	What are they using for tables? How about plates?
My teacher made me write "I will not eat my homework" ten times. When I was finished, I ate that too.	Adult: Where does it look like this worm is sitting? Yes, it looks like he's writing at his desk at school.

Notice how the adult in the extratextual conversation incorporates a few subtle questions and comments related to the setting. These comments and questions draw attention to the setting and show children the value of talking about the setting in which a story takes place. Hearing such questions and comments will likely prompt children to include similar details in the stories that they share with others.

Look Who's Talking

Objective: To discuss reported speech used by characters in a story

Storybook: *The Giant Carrot* (1998) by Jan Peck

Description: A family plants a carrot seed and helps care for it as they describe what they would like to make with the carrot once it has grown. This book uses reported speech on each page.

In this activity, we focus on *reported speech*, which describes what characters say in a story. Children's understanding of reported speech is closely tied to the developmental ability to recognize the mental states and verbal abilities of others (Greenhalgh & Strong, 2001). As children develop this ability, it is important for adults to discuss with children the thoughts that others have and the ways in which they use language to convey thoughts. Text bubbles, like those used in comic strips, are perfect for introducing children to the idea that language conveys mental states and verbal abilities.

Interactive Reading Experience Using *The Giant Carrot*

Text	Extratextual Conversation
(p. 3)	
Up walked strong Brother Abel. "Whatcha doin', Mama Bess?" "Plantin' a carrot seed, so come summer, I'll have a wide bowl of carrot stew."	Adult: Brother Abel, Mama Bess, and Papa Joe are all talking to one another on this page. I will use different voices for each of the characters so you can hear the difference. See these quotation marks around the words?

77

Brother Abel dipped a bucket into the well. He carried water to where Mama Bess had planted the seed. He scooped the water in his strong hands and sprinkled it over the soil.
"I've got my mouth set on a jar of strong carrot relish," he said.
Mama Bess and Papa Joe shook their heads.
"No," Papa Joe said, "I want a tall glass of carrot juice."
"No," Mama Bess said, "I want a wide bowl of carrot stew."

[points to the quotation marks (" ")] They tell us that someone in the book is talking. Can you show me any more sets of quotation marks on this page?

The Giant Carrot is used here for introducing the concept of reported speech because so many family members have different opinions about the same topic. Quotation marks in the story provide a visual cue for children that one of the characters is talking. Focusing on reported speech in storybook reading sessions is useful for developing the child's understanding that print can convey a character's message and also provides an important activity for building children's understanding of multiple perspectives. For instance, a child looking through The Giant Carrot might point to Mama Bess and say, "Mama Bess says, 'I want a wide bowl of carrot stew.'" Here, we use the global term of reported speech to describe the child's productions of both direct quotations ("I want a wide bowl of carrot stew") and dialogue carriers (Mama Bess says...). Experts suggest that children's understanding and production of reported speech demonstrate their familiarity with the written language register (Kaderavek & Sulzby, 2000). In contrast with the oral language register that we use in everyday conversations, the written language register is specific to the language of storybooks and the world of literacy. One key feature of this written language register is reported speech, and children's understanding and use of reported speech shows their developing familiarity with literate language.

ACTIVITY 6.5

Where the Excitement Is

Objective: To identify the high point of a story

Storybook: Clifford's Birthday Party (1988) by Norman Bridwell

Description: Clifford enjoys receiving lots of nice birthday gifts, but he realizes that the best gift of all is having his family and friends with him.

This activity focuses on plot in order to identify the high point in the story. Children with developing narrative abilities may fail to include a true high point in their narratives. Highlighting the high point in a storybook is one way to help children understand and begin to construct purposeful narratives.

Interactive Reading Experience Using *Clifford's Birthday Party*

Text	Extratextual Conversation
(pp. 27–30)	
Then came the cake. Clifford was surprised. He was even more surprised...	Adult: What do you think will happen with the cake? What do you think Clifford will be surprised by?
When his family popped out!	Adult: Wow, it's Clifford's family. He is so surprised and happy to see them.
He hadn't seen his mother and father and sisters and brother for a long time.	Adult: Why is Clifford so happy to see his family? He hasn't seen them in a long time. It's like when you get excited to see your grandmom after you haven't seen her for a while.
Clifford liked the presents his friends gave him, but having his family and friends with him was the best birthday present of all.	Adult: What was your favorite part of the story? Why did you like that part? What part of the story was the happiest for Clifford?

Experts have long tried to understand what makes a story a "good" story (e.g., McCabe & Peterson, 1984), as everyone seems to know a good story from a bad story. Many experts contend that what makes a story a good story is the inclusion of a suspension point, or a crisis that is subsequently resolved, also known as the "high point" (Labov, 1972). A good story is one which builds up strategically to a high point where the action suspends. At the high point, the narrative then moves to a resolution (McCabe & Peterson, 1984). Readers who have listened to young children's narratives recognize that immature narratives often do not have a high point, or they may achieve a high point that is not resolved. Adults can expose children to stories with a strong high point to build their awareness of story structure. *Clifford's Birthday Party* is a storybook with a simple plot yet a clear high point; thus, children should be able to identify and discuss the high point of the story with relative ease. Notice that the adult in the transcript emphasizes the high point of the story by asking the children to identify it and to describe how the main character feels during the high point of the story. When children are unable to identify the high point of a story, adults may ask them what their favorite part was and why. This strategy still allows children to select a section of the story that they found exciting and to elaborate on their feelings about that section.

Additional Storybooks for Building Narrative Knowledge

Cloudy With a Chance of Meatballs (1978) by Judi Barrett, illustrated by Ron Barrett

A grandfather tells a bedtime story to his grandchildren and helps them imagine what it would be like if food dropped like rain from the sky. This book is a good choice for highlighting the sequence of events in a story. It contains several time phrases, including *the next day*, *another day*, *seconds later*, *after*, and *that night*.

Corduroy (1968) by Don Freeman

Corduroy is a bear that has been waiting for a child to take him home from the store. He even attempts to fix himself up, by searching for a new button, so that someone will want to buy him. A young girl finally takes Corduroy home, giving Corduroy the home and friend he has always wanted. Adults can use this book to introduce children to the concept of plot. They can follow Corduroy's adventure as he goes in search of a new button and eventually finds a home and loving friend at the high point of the story.

The Gingerbread Boy (1997) by Richard Egielski

A gingerbread boy jumps out of the kitchen window straight from the oven and begins to run as several people in search of a snack chase after him. This book has wonderfully detailed pictures of a city, from the musicians in the subway station to the pedestrians walking below construction scaffolding, and is great for focusing on setting.

Good Night, Gorilla (1994) by Peggy Rathmann

A gorilla follows a zookeeper through the zoo and quietly unlocks all of the animals' cages. All of the animals end up in the zookeeper's bedroom, and when his wife notices, she leads all of the animals back to their cages. This book is useful for focusing on characters and what happens to them in a story. Adults can talk about the mischievous gorilla, the tired zookeeper, and his helpful wife, as well as how the actions of each of the characters make the story funny.

My Truck Is Stuck! (2002) by Kevin Lewis and Daniel Kirk

A truck-driving dog with a load of bones becomes stuck in a hole in the road. In a series of rhyming verses, dogs in various types of vehicles team up to free the stuck truck so that the important delivery can be made. Adults can use this story to focus on a story's characters and what happens to them. This book is also appropriate for illustrating environmental print, as several objects on the pages are labeled (e.g., *school bus*, *telephone*, *license plates*, *moving truck*).

A Penguin Pup for Pinkerton (2001) by Steven Kellogg

Pinkerton the dog dreams of adopting his own penguin and begins to treat a football that he found one day as if it were a penguin egg. This book is great for focusing on the sequence of events in a story, and it uses several adverbs and time phrases, including *today*, *almost*, *tomorrow*, *this afternoon*, and *yesterday*.

The Runaway Bunny (1942) by Margaret Wise Brown, illustrated by Clement Hurd

A little bunny decides that he wants to run away from home and tries to think of clever ways to escape. His mother responds by thinking of creative ways she would catch him if he were to run away. This book contains reported speech, which should be explicitly introduced to children so that they will incorporate it in their own personal narratives.

The Snowy Day (1962) by Ezra Jack Keats

This story conveys the excitement of a child's first snowfall. This story is appropriate for focusing on setting. We hear about the boy's adventures and his feelings as he moves from his bedroom to the street, to a hill of snow, back to his warm home, to the bathtub, into bed, and back out into the deep snow the next day.

We're Going on a Bear Hunt (1992) by Michael Rosen

Four children, along with their father and dog, go out in search of a bear. They must endure tall grass; a deep, cold river; thick mud; and a big, dark forest before finally finding a bear. Upon seeing the bear they are scared into retracing their steps back to where they began. Adults can use this book to focus on the high point of a story. Suspense builds as the children go in search of the bear, and the excitement reaches its peak when they finally find one.

Zug the Bug (1995) by Colin and Jacqui Hawkins

Zug the bug and a dog named Pug go fishing but instead catch a big, fat slug. This book has speech bubbles on each page that are great for introducing the concept of reported speech and how characters' speech is represented visually. Each page also features a different word that ends in -*ug*, so it is also perfect for focusing on rhymes.

This chapter has described interactive strategies for supporting children's development of narrative knowledge. In understanding and producing narratives, children must integrate many language domains, such as morphology, syntax, semantics, and pragmatics. Interactive strategies emphasized in this chapter target the child's attention to the sequence of events in a story, story characters, setting, reported speech that characters use, and the high point of a story. By repeatedly modeling these narrative conventions, adults can encourage children to include similarly detailed information in their own personal and fictional narratives, so as to make their stories more comprehensible and enjoyable for the listener. Chapter 7, on building world knowledge, further supports children's language acquisition during the early years of development to help children learn and apply concepts with which they might not yet be familiar.

CHAPTER 7

Building World Knowledge: Learning About the World Near and Far

As children develop, their knowledge of the world around them grows. This knowledge base includes children's understanding of concepts such as cultural diversity, money, character, nature, and life issues such as birth, death, and divorce. Children's development of language and literacy skills is linked to their broader knowledge base concerning the world in which they live. As children develop language and literacy, learning about the world around them becomes an important goal. The more experiences children have, the easier it is for them to assimilate new knowledge with what they already know. Books provide a key vehicle for introducing children to new experiences.

How World Knowledge Develops

Children develop their knowledge of the world around them as they interact with their environment directly and indirectly. The direct experiences children have in their homes, schools, and communities certainly provide the greatest amount of input to the world knowledge base. Much of this knowledge base is developed incidentally without direct instruction. For instance, the child whose commute to the main road takes her along a bumpy, gravel driveway with cows on either side incidentally develops a world map in which driveways embody these characteristics. For this child to develop an understanding of driveways that is more encompassing—in which driveways can be cement, blacktop, dirt, or gravel—she must experience many different driveways either through her own travels, through conversations with others, or through various media, such as movies, television shows, and storybooks. Certainly, driveways are just one tiny and relatively unimportant aspect of the child's world; however, this example does illustrate how children need experiences that reflect the larger world in which they live.

In considering how children develop their knowledge of the world, it is important to recognize that much of what children learn about the world is achieved within the context of their relationships with others. This perspective of world knowledge development views children as developing within a larger system, to include their family, their school, and their community, among other elements. Each system provides an important context for development (Pianta, 1999; Sameroff, 1989). As shown in Figure 1, children develop some world knowledge on their own (Path A), but much of this knowledge is achieved through their relationships with others (Path B). While thinking about specific knowledge to share with children is important, it is probably more important that educators focus on the quality of their relationships with children through which children will develop their knowledge of the world. That is, while educators should keep in mind the *what*—or the specific world knowledge goals they want to impart to children, such as time, geography, or weather—they must also think carefully about the *how*—or the quality of the relationships with children through which they impart this knowledge.

High-quality relationships between adults and children are those characterized by high levels of communication, warmth, and involvement, whereas low-quality relationships are those with high levels of conflict, reliance, and annoyance (Pianta, 1999). The extent to which the systems in which children are developing are characterized by high-quality relationships has important implications for children's developmental outcomes, including world knowledge (Pianta, Nimetz, & Bennett, 1997). Children learn more readily when this learning occurs in warm, nurturing, and secure relationships with the adults in their lives. Helping parents to support their children's world knowledge in the home environment is an important goal of early education. On the next page, we provide some tips for parents to guide your efforts.

FIGURE 1
Paths to Development of World Knowledge

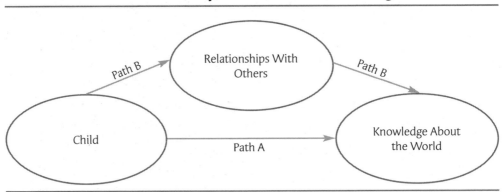

world Knowledge
Tips for parents

Parents can help their children to build world knowledge by drawing their attention to many aspects of the world around them. Take the opportunity during new experiences or special events to discuss and describe them. Also, introduce children to new vocabulary related to the experience. Here are some examples:

• Before an upcoming family reunion, discuss family heritage and customs. Share photos of relatives and explain how and when ancestors arrived in the United States.

• While hiking in the woods, take time to stop and explore plants and insects. Provide the specific names of different flora and fauna (e.g., oak, fern, daffodil, caterpillar, mosquito) to develop children's awareness of the many labels used to describe the world in which they live.

• Before taking a trip on an airplane, read about airplanes and airports. Introduce appropriate vocabulary like *runway*, *tarmac*, *luggage*, and *propeller*.

How Interactive Reading Supports the Development of World Knowledge

Children's worlds are relatively narrow, often involving their immediate home, community, and school. Storybooks provide an ideal context for introducing children to the larger world in which they live. For children who are raised on farms, storybooks can tell of urban and suburban culture (trains, buses, airports, museums, skyscrapers). Through storybooks, children in urban settings also learn about unique animals that inhabit ice caps, deserts, and jungles. The world knowledge topics available to children through interactive reading are amazingly numerous. Adults also guide children to experience books that incorporate a variety of concepts. Without adult guidance, children tend to select books that are familiar to them. More often than not, children select modern or traditional fantasy books over realistic fiction or informational books (Robinson, Larsen, Haupt, & Mohlman, 1997). It is important for parents and educators to expose children to a variety of genres covering a diverse assortment of topics.

Through various genres, adults can use books to open children's world to topics, concepts, and places to which they might otherwise not have access. Types of books useful for developing world knowledge include nonfiction books and poetry books. Parents and educators often do not consider nonfiction books when reading with younger children. However, nonfiction books provide a novel and effective way of introducing a child to the vocabulary that describes the world around them. For instance, the informational book, a form of nonfiction, is a genre that introduces or explains facts about many aspects of world knowledge. In addition to vocabulary, informational books can offer early access to the concepts, grammar, and structures of informational texts that children will encounter later in school, thus preparing them for a time when the focus shifts from learning to read to reading to learn (Smolkin & Donovan, 2003).

Poetry books, like nonfiction texts, are an underutilized genre in selecting storybooks to read with younger children. Poetry is well suited to introducing children to new vocabulary and new ways of thinking, particularly symbolic concepts like metaphors, similes, and proverbs. Poetry also differs from traditional fiction books and nonfiction books in its text structure, or the way in which text is organized to relay meaning. Experience with different text structures not only can help children understand how print varies in different texts but also can expose children more generally to the way in which various text structures share information about the world around them.

Interactive Reading Activities for Building World Knowledge

Here we present activities designed to encourage children's interest in topics and genres that will expand their world knowledge. In each activity, we will use a different genre to explore an aspect of world knowledge. Activities address the following objectives:

1. To demonstrate an understanding of the plant life cycle using an informational book in story format
2. To build vocabulary using an informational book and simple props
3. To describe the characteristics of unique animals using poetry
4. To build knowledge of signs using a book containing environmental print
5. To understand a variety of world cultures using a traditional storybook

Although many other aspects of world knowledge exist, these objectives are developmentally appropriate and exciting for young readers and provide points of reference from which to expand and explore knowledge of the world. At the end of this chapter, readers will find a list of additional books that illustrate concepts of world knowledge and represent the various genres discussed here.

A Tree of Knowledge

Objective: To demonstrate an understanding of the plant life cycle using an informational book in story format

Storybook: *Red Leaf, Yellow Leaf* (1991) by Lois Ehlert

Description: This informational book presents the life cycle of a tree in a story format from the point of view of a child. It introduces novel vocabulary related to tree and plant parts and is enhanced by the brilliantly colored collages that incorporate not only parts of real plants but also plastic, paper, wire, and ribbon. Although the bold story text is geared toward younger children, the object labels throughout the collage and the detailed information (nonfiction) about tree parts and tree planting at the end of the book extend the appeal of the book to children of all ages.

Red Leaf, Yellow Leaf includes many object labels and salient print. It provides an excellent opportunity to talk about the print as well as the story itself. While reading this storybook, adults are encouraged to use the following three strategies:

1. Repeat and define new vocabulary

2. Point to print labels

3. Track print while reading

Interactive Reading Experience Using *Red Leaf, Yellow Leaf*

Text (pp. 7–12)	Extratextual Conversation
	Adult: This book is about leaves and trees. Remember when we went camping and looked at different trees? This book will tell us how trees grow.
When spring sun warmed the seeds, they sprouted and sent roots down into the soil. Tiny leaves unfolded their stems.	Adult: The seeds *sprouted*. That means they started to grow.

I think my tree would've been happy to stay there forever. But one day nursery workers came to the woods to collect tree sprouts.	Adult: A *nursery worker* is a person who works in a tree nursery. A *tree nursery* is where trees are grown.
They transplanted the sprouts and tended them year after year.	Adult: There's the word *sprouts* again! They tended them year [points to *year*] after year [points to *year*].

The combinations of art and objects in *Red Leaf, Yellow Leaf* make the illustrations intriguing. In the preceding example of an interactive reading, the child is listening intently while the adult leaves the text periodically to expose the child to key vocabulary concepts, like *nursery* and *sprout*, and to link the text to the child's own experiences with camping. The adult asks the child few questions and does not prompt the child to participate during this first exposure to these novel concepts. With future readings, the adult can prompt children to remember how they learned about the topic of trees and growth.

If I Had a Hammer

Objective: To build vocabulary using an informational book and simple props

Storybook: *Tools* (1998) by Ann Morris, illustrated by Ken Heyman

Description: This book presents a variety of tools and their unique uses. Some of these tools will be familiar to children, and others will offer opportunities to compare and contrast familiar with unfamiliar.

While reading this storybook, adults are encouraged to use the following three strategies:

1. Show props to illustrate new vocabulary
2. Use adjectives and descriptions to label objects, attributes, and actions shown in the illustrations
3. Use open-ended questions to encourage dialogue

Interactive Reading Experience Using *Tools*

Text (pp. 16–23)	Extratextual Conversation
	[Adult previews the book and finds some readily available props similar to the tools in the book.]

We even eat with tools	Adult: Here are some tools that we eat with. Can you find the *spoon*?
	Adult: That little girl is eating with *chopsticks*. See [points to picture], they're sticks that you use to eat.
People use tools to make things	Adult: He's pounding with a *hammer*. His hammer is big. Mommy's hammer is small.
And to fix things	Adult: They are fixing the *red net*. Why do you think they use the red net?
And to clean	Adult: What is he going to do with the *cart*?

In the preceding extratextual conversation, the adult uses physical props to illustrate and contrast the vocabulary encountered in the text during the reading. The child has the opportunity to link the text to real objects. During the initial reading, the adult can emphasize the vocabulary and the different uses of the tools. For subsequent readings, discussion can be initiated regarding the different cultural elements that exist in the photographs. These elements can be compared and contrasted with the child's immediate environment, further building world knowledge.

A Whale of a Tale

Objective: To describe the characteristics of unique animals using poetry

Storybook: *Beast Feast* (1994) by Douglas Florian

Description: This book is ideal for reading aloud. It presents an array of exotic animals through a series of short and quirky poems. In addition to exposing children to poetry, adults have the opportunity to teach about a variety of animals and their environments, habits, or characteristics.

While reading this storybook, adults are encouraged to use the following three strategies:

1. Emphasize rhyming words
2. Use open-ended questions to encourage dialogue about the topic of the poem
3. Repeat and define new vocabulary

Interactive Reading Experience Using *Beast Feast*

Text	Extratextual Conversation
("The Whale," p. 23)	[Adult first reads the poem once through.]
	Listen to the words that rhyme in this poem. *Street/feet, blubber/rubber, out/spout, shore/more/ignore.*
Big as a street— *With fins, not feet—* *...*	Look at the picture of the whale. The poem says, he has "fins, not feet." Where do you think his *fins* are? Why do you think he has *fins* instead of *feet*?
When I breathe out, *I spew a spout.*	He spews water out of a hole in the top of his head. The hole is called a *spout. Spew* means to spray. Look how the letters in the word *spew* are *sprayed* on the page!

In addition to providing the child with exposure to a new genre, poetry can be used to reinforce rhyme awareness and rhyme production. During the preceding extratextual conversation, the adult first reads the poem to the child and then, during a second reading, prompts the child to think about and identify rhymes in the poem. The adult also uses open-ended questions to discuss the whale and further involve the child in the reading interaction.

ACTIVITY 7.4

Signs, Signs, Everywhere a Sign

Objective: To build knowledge of signs using a book containing environmental print

Storybook: *I Read Signs* (1983) by Tana Hoban

Description: Children often recognize symbols and signs around them long before they can read. This book of photographed street signs provides an excellent opportunity to introduce the environmental print that is often one of the first reading accomplishments for children.

While reading this storybook, adults are encouraged to use the following three strategies:

1. Emphasize beginning sounds

2. Use open-ended questions to encourage dialogue

3. Explicitly reference print features, such as letters, repeated words, and text directionality

Interactive Reading Experience Using *I Read Signs*

Text (pp. 13–17)	Extratextual Conversation
STOP	Adult: *S-T* makes the /st/ sound. What do you think this sign says?
NO LEFT TURN	Adult: "No left turn." Which way do you think is *left*?
KEEP RIGHT	Adult: "Keep right." Why do you think the arrow is pointing that way?
EXIT	Adult: *E-X-I-T.* Can you find an *X* on the next page?
NO STANDING—EXPRESS	Adult: "No standing." *N-O* spells *no*. Let's look at all of the pages to see if we can find some other signs that say "No."

During the preceding extratextual conversation, the adult uses many of the techniques discussed in previous chapters. Explicit references are made to beginning sounds and print features. The adult also exposes the child to environmental print in an interactive manner that may enhance the child's ability to recognize the print later in decontextualized situations (Vukelich, 1994).

ACTIVITY 7.5

An Alphabetic Tour

Objective: To understand a variety of world cultures using a traditional storybook

Storybook: *Away From Home* by Anita Lobel (1994)

Description: With an alphabetic tour of the world from Amsterdam to Zaandam, the illustrations of each locale include hints as to the costumes and customs of its residents. Adults can help children to explore the illustrations to discover the world far away.

While reading this storybook, adults are encouraged to use the following three strategies:

1. Comment on the beginning sounds of the words beginning with each letter

2. Reference print (point out features and functions of the print)

3. Ask open-ended questions about the people and places in the story

Interactive Reading Experience Using *Away From Home*

Text (pp. 1–10)	Extratextual Conversation
Edward escaped in Edinburgh.	Adult: Edward left Edinburgh. Edinburgh is in Scotland. Why did Edward leave?
Frederick fiddled in Florence.	Adult: Look at all of those words that begin with *F*. Can you think of some other words that begin with *F*?
Garret gazed in Giza.	Adult: What do you think Garret saw when he gazed in Giza?

During the preceding extratextual conversation, the adult is reinforcing alphabet knowledge and beginning sounds. Alphabet books such as *Away From Home* provide a wonderful opportunity to reference specific letters, and print in general. The global content of this book also provides an opportunity to extend world knowledge through conversation about each of the people and places mentioned.

Additional Storybooks for Building World Knowledge

In recommending additional storybooks for building world knowledge, we have included a variety of genres. We have organized by area of world knowledge the book best supports from the following categories:

- Animals and Nature
- Character and Values
- Life Issues
- Money, Time, and Numbers
- People, Places, and Cultures

Animals and Nature

Growing Vegetable Soup (1987) by Lois Ehlert

This book features illustrations in bold colors and a story written in large, salient print. In addition to the story text, print is used to label illustrations on each page. The story moves step-by-step through planting, growing, harvesting, preparing, and eating the vegetables grown in a garden and includes instructions on how to make your own vegetable soup.

Mama Zooms (1993) by Jane Cowen-Fletcher

This story captures the imagination of a little boy whose mother is in a wheelchair. He views the wheelchair not as an obstacle, but as a zooming machine. Riding with Mama on the zooming machine, he is a jockey, a sea captain, a train engineer, and more.

The Rain Came Down (2000) by David Shannon

Using this delightfully illustrated story, adults can introduce children to the changes of weather as well as the changes of mood that occur in the story.

Where Do Bears Sleep? (1970) by Barbara Shook Hazen, illustrated by Ian E. Staunton

This book presents the sleeping habitats of a variety of animals through rhyming text. While some of the animals may be familiar, others will be new to children.

Character and Values

Fish Is Fish (1970) by Leo Lionni

This story of a tadpole and a fish illustrates how friends may change, but the friendship can remain. After the tadpole grows into a frog and spends some time on land, he returns to the water to share his adventures with his friend the fish. The book teaches a lesson about being happy with who you are.

The Missing Piece (1976) by Shel Silverstein

Using simple line drawings, Shel Silverstein tells a story that provides an opportunity to discuss self-esteem.

Swimmy (1973) by Leo Lionni

A small black fish in the great, big sea uses creative thinking and problem-solving skills to help his friends move freely among their foes. The story wonderfully illustrates how being different can be a positive thing and how problems can be solved by working together.

Life Issues

Charlie Anderson (1990) by Barbara Abercrombie, illustrated by Mark Graham

The adorable cat, Charlie Anderson, has two homes just like Elizabeth and Sarah. The surprise behind Charlie's two homes presents a wonderful opportunity to discuss separation or divorce with young children.

The Kissing Hand (1993) by Audrey Penn, illustrated by Ruth E. Harper and Nancy M. Leak

As Mrs. Raccoon explains in the story, "Sometimes we all have to do things we don't want to do, even if they seem strange and scary at first" (p. 3). Mrs. Raccoon goes on to share with her son a secret kiss that he can take with him to use whenever he needs reassurance or a reminder of her love. This wonderful story can be applied to many situations in which children will have to confront something difficult or scary.

Money, Time, and Numbers

Count! (1992) by Denise Fleming

Count to 10, 20, 30, 40, and 50. This colorfully illustrated book introduces some interesting animals while teaching or reinforcing counting skills. Tick marks are included to count with pictures.

10 Minutes Till Bedtime (1998) by Peggy Rathmann

The countdown to bedtime has come, and the hamster parade begins. This book has very little story text but many salient print elements and intricate illustrations that provide for much discussion. Set a timer for 10 minutes and reinforce the concept of time while reading.

12 Ways to Get to 11 (1993) by Eve Merriam, illustrated by Bernie Karlin

This counting book is not only useful to focus on the concept of counting; it can also be used to support the concepts of likeness, similarity, and sorting. The book provides a number of ways to count to 11, each using a creative combination of related items.

People, Places, and Cultures

Bringing the Rain to Kapiti Plain (1981) by Verna Aardema, illustrated by Beatriz Vidal

The cumulative refrain in this book ("the cloud, all heavy with rain, that shadowed the ground of Kapiti Plain") offers a wonderful opportunity for child participation in the storybook reading. This African folk tale was originally discovered in Kenya more than 70 years ago. Aardema has written her version of the tale using rhyme and rhythm similar to the more traditional "The House That Jack Built."

Mapping Penny's World (2000) by Loreen Leedy

As a school project, Lisa maps the world inhabited by her Boston terrier, Penny. The story includes narrative descriptions of environments encountered by Penny, followed by Lisa's map of the environment. The maps provide lots of salient print, symbols, and associated labels.

My Big Book of Everything (1996) by Roger Priddy

This book of colorful photographs provides pictures and labels for over 600 items. The photos are grouped by theme and provide wonderful opportunities to discuss and illustrate new vocabulary for everything from clothes to household items, occupations to animals, and much more.

This chapter has described interactive strategies for supporting children's developing world knowledge by introducing activities that explore the plant life cycle, build vocabulary of tools, describe characteristics of animals, build knowledge of signs, and describe a variety of world cultures. The activities in this chapter have encouraged adults to consider multiple book genres, including poetry, nonfiction informational books, and to augment storybook readings with simple props.

CONCLUSION

Accelerating children's language and literacy development through interactive storybook reading can be both fun and effective. This book has presented a variety of developmentally appropriate and evidence-based activities designed to foster children's development in print knowledge, word knowledge, phonological knowledge, alphabet knowledge, narrative knowledge, and world knowledge. Collectively, these aspects of early language and literacy development help children develop a strong foundation that will prepare them to be successful readers during the early and later years of formal schooling. As several of the storybooks in our activities would be useful to foster multiple areas of language and literacy development, this book also includes an appendix that adults can consult in order to get double-duty out of the storybooks that we suggest. Educators and other professionals who have a stake in fostering children's early language and literacy can use these activities to scaffold with storybooks so that children will continue to build the important readiness skills that will equip them to meet the academic challenges that await them in the early elementary years.

Cross-Referencing List
of All Storybooks

This appendix contains the names of storybooks referenced in each chapter. The 📖 icon has been used to denote those concepts that are best illustrated or supported by the corresponding book. Although many of the concepts introduced throughout the chapters of this book can be supported using any storybook, we have chosen to designate books that have the most salient features for supporting each concept. For instance, any book can be used to reinforce the concept of text directionality, but books with limited amounts of larger print are particularly well suited to focusing on this concept.

	Alphabet and Print Awareness		Word Knowledge				Phonological Knowledge					Narrative Knowledge				
	Letters and their attributes	Text directionality	Actions in the story	Emotions	Adjectives	Prepositions and opposites	Word counting	Segmenting / blending	Rhyme awareness	Beginning sounds	Final sounds	Concept of time words	Characters	Setting	Reported speech	Concept of plot
10 Minutes Till Bedtime (1998) by Peggy Rathmann	📖	📖	📖				📖					📖				
12 Ways to Get to 11 (1993) by Eve Merriam	📖	📖					📖									
26 Letters and 99 Cents (1987) by Tana Hoban	📖															
A to Z, Do You Ever Feel Like Me? A Guessing Alphabet of Feelings, Words, and Other Cool Stuff (1999) by Bonnie Hausman	📖			📖												

Away From Home (1994) by Anita Lobel	📖									📖						
The Awful Aardvarks Go to School (1997) by Reeve Lindbergh	📖	📖	📖		📖	📖	📖	📖	📖	📖			📖			
Bear Snores On (2001) by Karma Wilson			📖	📖					📖					📖		
Beast Feast (1994) by Douglas Florian									📖	📖	📖					
The Berenstain Bears Ready, Get Set, Go! (1988) by Stan Berenstain & Jan Berenstain			📖		📖											
The Big Hat (1999) by Bobby Lynn Maslen		📖					📖		📖		📖					
Bringing the Rain to Kapiti Plain (1981) by Verna Aardema									📖			📖		📖		
Brown Bear, Brown Bear What Do You See? (1992) by Bill Martin Jr	📖	📖					📖		📖							
Busy, Busy Mouse (2003) by Virginia Kroll	📖	📖	📖			📖	📖		📖					📖		

(continued)

	Alphabet and Print Awareness		Word Knowledge				Phonological Awareness					Narrative Knowledge				
	Letters and their attributes	Text directionality	Actions in the story	Emotions	Adjectives	Prepositions and opposites	Word counting	Segmenting / blending	Rhyme awareness	Beginning sounds	Final sounds	Concept of time words	Characters	Setting	Reported speech	Concept of plot
Calico Cat at the Zoo (1981) by Donald Charles					☑				☑							
Charlie Anderson (1990) by Barbara Abercrombie												☑	☑	☑	☑	☑
Chicka Chicka Boom Boom (1989) by Bill Martin Jr & John Archambault	☑	☑							☑							
Clifford's Birthday (1988) by Norman Bridwell													☑	☑		☑
Cloudy With a Chance of Meatballs (1978) by Judi Barrett												☑				☑

| Come Along, Daisy! (1998) by Jane Simmons |
| Corduroy (1968) by Don Freeman |
| Count! (1992) by Denise Fleming |
| David Gets in Trouble (2002) by David Shannon |
| Dear Mrs. LaRue: Letters from Obedience School (2002) by Mark Teague |
| Dear Zoo (1982) by Rod Campbell |
| Diary of a Worm (2003) by Doreen Cronin |
| Don't Let the Pigeon Drive the Bus! (2003) by Mo Willems |
| Elephants Aloft (1993) by Kathi Appelt |
| Exactly the Opposite (1990) by Tana Hoban |

(continued)

Book	Alphabet and Print Awareness		Word Knowledge				Phonological Awareness					Narrative Knowledge				
	Letters and their attributes	Text directionality	Actions in the story	Emotions	Adjectives	Prepositions and opposites	Word counting	Segmenting / blending	Rhyme awareness	Beginning sounds	Final sounds	Concept of time words	Characters	Setting	Reported speech	Concept of plot
Fall Leaves Fall! (2000) by Zoe Hall	▦															
Fish Is Fish (1970) by Leo Lionni				▦												
The Foot Book (1968/2002) by Dr. Seuss					▦	▦										
Freight Train (1978) by Donald Crews	▦	▦	▦		▦	▦	▦	▦				▦		▦		
Froggy Gets Dressed (1992) by Jonathan London								▦		▦						
Froggy Plays Soccer (1999) by Jonathan London	▦							▦		▦						

Title																
The Giant Carrot (1998) by Jan Peck																📖
The Gingerbread Boy (1997) by Richard Egielski	📖	📖													📖	
Good Night, Gorilla (1994) by Peggy Rathmann	📖	📖	📖		📖								📖			
Goose on the Loose (2001) by Phil Roxbee Cox					📖		📖	📖				📖				
Growing Vegetable Soup (1987) by Lois Ehlert	📖	📖		📖	📖											
How Are You Peeling? Foods With Moods (1999) by Saxton Freymann & Joost Elffers			📖													
How Big Is a Pig? (2000) by Clare Beaton				📖												
Hug (2000) by Jez Alborough	📖		📖	📖												
I Read Signs (1983) by Tana Hoban	📖				📖					📖		📖				
I Went Walking (1990) by Sue Williams		📖	📖		📖	📖										

(continued)

103

	Alphabet and Print Awareness		Word Knowledge				Phonological Awareness					Narrative Knowledge				
	Letters and their attributes	Text directionality	Actions in the story	Emotions	Adjectives	Prepositions and opposites	Word counting	Segmenting / blending	Rhyme awareness	Beginning sounds	Final sounds	Concept of time words	Characters	Setting	Reported speech	Concept of plot
If You Give a Moose a Muffin (1991) by Laura Numeroff	▣	▣	▣										▣	▣		▣
If You Give a Mouse a Cookie (1985) by Laura Numeroff	▣	▣	▣										▣	▣		▣
If You Give a Pig a Pancake (1998) by Laura Numeroff	▣	▣	▣					▣					▣	▣		▣
In the Small, Small Pond (1993) by Denise Fleming	▣	▣							▣					▣		
In the Tall, Tall Grass (1991) by Denise Fleming	▣	▣							▣	▣				▣		

Jiggle, Wiggle, Prance (1987) by Sally Noll				📖						📖							
The Kissing Hand (1993) by Audrey Penn		📖	📖	📖		📖								📖	📖		
Maisy at the Fair (2001) by Lucy Cousins	📖	📖													📖	📖	
Mama Cat Has Three Kittens (1998) by Denise Fleming	📖	📖		📖			📖			📖		📖	📖				
Mama Zooms (1993) by Jane Cowen-Fletcher			📖	📖										📖			
The Missing Piece (1976) by Shel Silverstein				📖				📖	📖								
Mr. Gumpy's Outing (1970) by John Burningham						📖					📖						
My Big Book of Everything (1996) by Roger Priddy																	
My Car (2001) by Byron Barton	📖	📖							📖								
My Street (1998) by Rebecca Treays	📖	📖				📖										📖	

(continued)

Book	Alphabet and Print Awareness		Word Knowledge				Phonological Awareness					Narrative Knowledge				
	Letters and their attributes	Text directionality	Actions in the story	Emotions	Adjectives	Prepositions and opposites	Word counting	Segmenting / blending	Rhyme awareness	Beginning sounds	Final sounds	Concept of time words	Characters	Setting	Reported speech	Concept of plot
My Truck Is Stuck (2002) by Kevin Lewis & Daniel Kirk	✓	✓	✓						✓				✓			
Nibbly Mouse (1994) by David Drew							✓			✓				✓		
A Penguin Pup for Pinkerton (2001) by Steven Kellogg												✓	✓	✓		✓
Pete's a Pizza (1998) by William Steig			✓										✓	✓		
The Rain Came Down (2000) by David Shannon			✓		✓											

(continued)

Title																
Red Leaf, Yellow Leaf (1991) by Lois Ehlert	⊟	⊟	⊟										⊟			
Rumble in the Jungle (1997) by Giles Andreae	⊟					⊟										
The Runaway Bunny (1942) by Margaret Wise Brown															⊟	
Sam Sheep Can't Sleep (2000) by Phil Roxbee Cox	⊟	⊟	⊟	⊟	⊟	⊟	⊟	⊟	⊟	⊟	⊟			⊟	⊟	
School Bus (1984) by Donald Crews	⊟	⊟	⊟	⊟				⊟						⊟		
Sheep in a Jeep (1986) by Nancy Shaw	⊟	⊟	⊟	⊟	⊟	⊟	⊟	⊟								
Sheep in a Shop (1991) by Nancy Shaw		⊟		⊟	⊟											
Sheep Out to Eat (1992) by Nancy Shaw			⊟	⊟	⊟											
The Snowy Day (1962) by Ezra Jack Keats		⊟										⊟	⊟			
Sometimes I'm Bombaloo (2002) by Rachel Vail			⊟										⊟			

	Alphabet and Print Awareness		Word Knowledge				Phonological Awareness					Narrative Knowledge				
	Letters and their attributes	Text directionality	Actions in the story	Emotions	Adjectives	Prepositions and opposites	Word counting	Segmenting / blending	Rhyme awareness	Beginning sounds	Final sounds	Concept of time words	Characters	Setting	Reported speech	Concept of plot
Spot Goes to the Farm (1987) by Eric Hill	📖	📖					📖							📖	📖	
Spot's First Walk (1981) by Eric Hill	📖	📖	📖		📖	📖	📖						📖	📖	📖	
Super, Super, Superwords (1989) by Bruce Mcmillan					📖	📖										
Swimmy (1973) by Leo Lionni		📖		📖				📖					📖	📖		📖
There Was an Old Lady Who Swallowed a Fly (1997) by Simms Taback													📖		📖	📖

Title													
They Call Me Woolly: What Animal Names Can Tell Us (2002) by Keith DuQuette					⊞							⊞	
This Old Man (2000), illustrated by Carol Jones	⊞	⊞	⊞		⊞	⊞		⊞		⊞			⊞
Tools (1998) by Ann Morris			⊞										
Top Cat (1998) by Lois Ehlert	⊞	⊞	⊞			⊞	⊞	⊞			⊞	⊞	
Trucks, Trucks, Trucks (1999) by Peter Sis			⊞										
The Very Busy Spider (1984) by Eric Carle	⊞		⊞	⊞	⊞								
The Very Hungry Caterpillar (1994) by Eric Carle					⊞							⊞	
Watch William Walk (1997) by Ann Jonas							⊞						
We're Going on a Bear Hunt (1992) by Michael Rosen	⊞	⊞									⊞	⊞	⊞
Where Do Bears Sleep? (1970) by Barbara Shook Hazen				⊞								⊞	

(continued)

	Alphabet and Print Awareness		Word Knowledge				Phonological Awareness					Narrative Knowledge				
	Letters and their attributes	Text directionality	Actions in the story	Emotions	Adjectives	Prepositions and opposites	Word counting	Segmenting / blending	Rhyme awareness	Beginning sounds	Final sounds	Concept of time words	Characters	Setting	Reported speech	Concept of plot
Where's Curly? (2003) by Heather Amery							📖							📖	📖	
Zin! Zin! Zin! Violin (1995) by Lloyd Moss								📖	📖							
Zug the Bug (1995) by Colin Hawkins and Jacqui Hawkins									📖		📖				📖	

REFERENCES

Adams, M.J. (1990). *Beginning to read: Thinking and learning about print.* Cambridge, MA: MIT Press.

Anthony, J.L., Lonigan, C.J., Driscoll, K., Phillips, B.M., & Burgess, S.R. (2003). Phonological sensitivity: A quasi-parallel progression of word structure units and cognitive operations. *Reading Research Quarterly, 38*(4), 470–487.

Bailey, D. (1989). Assessment and its importance in early intervention. In D.B. Bailey & M. Wolery (Eds.), *Assessing infants and preschoolers with handicaps* (pp. 1–21). Columbus, OH: Merrill.

Bear, D.R., Invernizzi, M., Templeton, S., & Johnston, F. (2004). *Words their way: Word study for phonics, vocabulary, and spelling instruction* (3rd ed.). Upper Saddle River, NJ: Pearson/Merrill/Prentice Hall.

Beck, I.L., McKeown, M.G., & Kucan, L. (2002). *Bringing words to life.* New York: Guilford Press.

Berko Gleason, J. (2005). *The development of language* (6th ed.). Boston: Pearson/Allyn & Bacon.

Bowey, J.A. (1995). Socioeconomic status differences in preschool phonological sensitivity and first-grade reading achievement. *Journal of Educational Psychology, 87*(3), 476–487.

Brown, R. (1973). *A first language: The early stages.* Cambridge, MA: Harvard University Press.

Bruner, J.S. (1978). The role of dialogue in language acquisition. In A. Sinclair, R.J. Jarvelle, & W.J.M. Levelt (Eds.), *The child's conception of language* (pp. 241–256). New York: Springer-Verlag.

Burns, M.S., Griffin, P., & Snow, C.E. (Eds.). (1999). *Starting out right: A guide to promoting children's reading success.* Washington, DC: National Academy Press.

Bus, A.G. (2001). Joint caregiver-child storybook reading: A route to literacy development. In S.B. Neuman & D.K. Dickinson (Eds.), *Handbook of early literacy research* (pp. 179–191). New York: Guilford Press.

Bus, A.G., & Van IJzendoorn, M.H. (1995). Mothers reading to their 3-year-olds—The role of mother-child attachment security in becoming literate. *Reading Research Quarterly, 30*(4), 998–1015.

Carroll, J.M., Snowling, M.J., Hulme, C., & Stevenson, J. (2003). The development of phonological awareness in preschool children. *Developmental Psychology, 39*(5), 913–923.

Catts, H.W., Fey, M.E., Tomblin, J.B., & Zhang, X. (2002). A longitudinal investigation of reading outcomes in children with language impairments. *Journal of Speech, Language, & Hearing Research, 45*(6), 1142–1157.

Chall, J.S. (1983). *Stages of reading development.* New York: McGraw-Hill.

Chaney, C. (1994). Language development, metalinguistic awareness, and emergent literacy skills of 3-year-old children in relation to social class. *Applied Psycholinguistics, 15*(3), 371–394.

Chaney, C. (1998). Preschool language and metalinguistic skills are links to reading success. *Applied Psycholinguistics, 19*(3), 433–446.

Choi, S. (2000). Caregiver input in English and Korean: Use of nouns and verbs in book-reading and toy-play contexts. *Journal of Child Language, 27*(1), 69–96.

Choi, S., & Gopnik, A. (1995). Early acquisition of verbs in Korean: A cross-linguistic study. *Journal of Child Language, 22*(3), 497–529.

Crain-Thoreson, C., & Dale, P.S. (1999). Enhancing linguistic performance: Parents and teachers as book reading partners for children with language delays. *Topics in Early Childhood Special Education, 19*(1), 28–39.

Curenton, S., & Justice, L.M. (2004). African American and Caucasian preschoolers' use of decontextualized language: Literate language features in oral narratives. *Language, Speech, & Hearing Services in Schools, 35*(3), 240–253.

Diaz, R.M., Neal, C., & Vachio, A. (1990). Maternal teaching in the zone of proximal development: A comparison of low- and high-risk dyads. *Merrill-Palmer Quarterly, 37*(1), 83–107.

Dickinson, D.K., & Keebler, R. (1989). Variation in preschool teachers' storybook reading styles. *Discourse Processes, 12*, 353–376.

Ehri, L. (1991). Learning to read and spell words. In L. Rieben & C.A. Perfetti (Eds.), *Learning to read: Basic research and its implications* (pp. 57–73). Hillsdale, NJ: Erlbaum.

Elley, W.B. (1989). Vocabulary acquisition from listening to stories. *Reading Research Quarterly, 24*(2), 174–187.

Ezell, H.K., & Justice, L.M. (1998). A pilot investigation of parent questions about print and pictures to preschoolers with language delay. *Child Language Teaching & Therapy, 14*, 273–278.

Ezell, H.K., & Justice, L.M. (2000). Increasing the print focus of shared reading through observational learning. *American Journal of Speech-Language Pathology, 9*, 36–47.

Fernandez-Fein, S., & Baker, L. (1997). Rhyme and alliteration sensitivity and relevant experiences among preschoolers from diverse backgrounds. *Journal of Literacy Research, 29*(3), 433–459.

Feuerstein, R. (1980). *Instrumental enrichment: An intervention program for cognitive modifiability.* Baltimore: University Park Press.

Fox, B., & Routh, D.K. (1975). Analyzing spoken language into words, syllables, and phonemes: A developmental study. *Journal of Psycholinguistic Research, 4*(4), 331–342.

Francis, D.J., Shaywitz, S.E., Stuebing, K.K., Shaywitz, B.A., & Fletcher, J.M. (1996). Developmental lag versus deficit models of reading disability: A longitudinal, individual growth curves analysis. *Journal of Educational Psychology, 88*(1), 3–17.

Fujiki, M., Brinton, B., & Clarke, D. (2002). Emotion regulation in children with specific language impairment. *Language, Speech, & Hearing Services in Schools, 33*(2), 102–111.

Ganger, J., & Brent, M.R. (2004). Reexamining the vocabulary spurt. *Developmental Psychology, 40*(4), 621–632.

Gentner, D. (1978). On relational meaning: The acquisition of verb meaning. *Child Development, 49*(4), 988–998.

Gentner, D. (1982). Why nouns are learned before verbs: Linguistic relativity versus natural partitioning. In S. Kuczaj II (Ed.), *Language development: Language, thought, and culture* (Vol. 2, pp. 301–334). Hillsdale, NJ: Erlbaum.

Girolametto, L., Pearce, P.S., & Weitzman, E. (1996). Interactive focused stimulation for toddlers with expressive vocabulary delays. *Journal of Speech and Hearing Research, 39*(6), 1274–1283.

Goldfield, B.A., & Reznick, J.S. (1990). Early lexical acquisition: Rate, content, and the vocabulary spurt. *Journal of Child Language, 17*(1), 171–183.

Goodman, Y.M. (1986). Children coming to know literacy. In W.H. Teale & E. Sulzby (Eds.), *Emergent literacy: Writing and reading* (pp. 1–14). Norwood, NJ: Ablex.

Goswami, U., & Bryant, P.E. (1990). *Phonological skills and learning to read.* Hillsdale, NJ: Erlbaum.

Gough, P.B., & Tunmer, W.E. (1986). Decoding, reading, and reading disability. *Remedial & Special Education, 7*(1), 6–10.

Greenfield, P.M. (1984). A theory of the teacher in the learning activities of everyday life. In B. Rogoff & J. Lave (Eds.), *Everyday cognition: Its development in social context* (pp. 117–138). Cambridge, MA: Harvard University Press.

Greenhalgh, K.S., & Strong, C.J. (2001). Literate language features in spoken narratives of children with typical language and children with language impairments. *Language, Speech, & Hearing Services in Schools, 32*(2), 114–125.

Hall, D.G. (1996). Preschoolers' default assumptions about word meaning: Proper names designate unique individuals. *Developmental Psychology, 32*(1), 177–186.

Hall, D.G., Burns, T.C., & Pawluski, J.L. (2003). Input and word learning: Caregivers' sensitivity to lexical category distinctions. *Journal of Child Language, 30*(3), 711–729.

Hammett, L.A., van Kleeck, A., & Huberty, C.J. (2003). Patterns of parents' extratextual interactions during book sharing with preschool children: A cluster analysis study. *Reading Research Quarterly, 38*(4), 442–468.

Hart, B., & Risley, T.R. (1995). *Meaningful differences in the everyday experiences of young American children*. Baltimore: Paul H. Brookes.

Hegde, M.N. (1985). *Treatment procedures in communicative disorders*. San Diego, CA: College-Hill Press.

Hiebert, E.H. (1981). Developmental patterns and interrelationships of preschool children's print awareness. *Reading Research Quarterly, 16*(2), 236–260.

Hoff, E. (2001). *Language development* (2nd ed.). Belmont, CA: Wadsworth/Thomson Learning.

Hoff, E., & Naigles, L. (2002). How children use input to acquire a lexicon. *Child Development, 73*(2), 418–433.

Hoff-Ginsberg, E. (1998). The relation of birth order and socioeconomic status to children's language experience and language development. *Applied Psycholinguistics, 19*(4), 603–629.

Hutchison, J.K. (2001). Telephone communications enhance children's narratives. *Dissertation Abstracts International, 63*(09). (Publication No. AAT NQ72449)

Imai, M., Haryu, E., & Okada, H. (2002). Is verb learning easier than noun learning for Japanese children? 3-year-old Japanese children's knowledge about object names and action names. In B. Skarabela, S. Fish, & A.H.J. Do (Eds.), *Proceedings of the 26th Annual Boston University Conference on Language Development: Vol. 1.* (pp. 324–335). Somerville, MA: Cascadilla Press.

Johnson, C. (2004). *Nation's report card: An overview of NAEP*. (NCES Publication No. 2004552). National Center for Education Statistics. Retrieved October 5, 2004, from http://nces.ed.gov/pubsearch/pubsinfo.asp?pubid=2004552

Juel, C. (1988). Learning to read and write: A longitudinal study of 54 children from first through fourth grades. *Journal of Educational Psychology, 80*(4), 437–447.

Justice, L.M. (2002). Word exposure conditions and preschoolers' novel word learning during shared storybook reading. *Reading Psychology, 23*(2), 87–106.

Justice, L.M., & Ezell, H.K. (2000). Enhancing children's print and word awareness through home-based parent intervention. *American Journal of Speech-Language Pathology, 9*, 257–269.

Justice, L.M., & Ezell, H.K. (2001). Written language awareness in preschool children from low-income households: A descriptive analysis. *Communication Disorders Quarterly, 22*(3), 123–134.

Justice, L.M., & Ezell, H.K. (2002). Use of storybook reading to increase print awareness in at-risk children. *American Journal of Speech-Language Pathology, 11*, 17–29.

Justice, L.M., & Ezell, H.K. (2004). Print referencing: An emergent literacy enhancement technique and its clinical applications. *Language, Speech, & Hearing Services in Schools, 35*(2), 185–193.

Justice, L.M., & Lankford, C. (2002). Preschool children's visual attention to print during storybook reading: Pilot findings. *Communication Disorders Quarterly, 24*(1), 11–21.

Justice, L.M., Meier, J., & Walpole, S. (2005). Learning new words from storybooks: An efficacy study with at-risk kindergartners. *Language, Speech, & Hearing Services in Schools, 36*, 17–32.

Justice, L.M., & Pullen, P.C. (2003). Promising interventions for promoting emergent literacy skills: Three evidence-based approaches. *Topics in Early Childhood Special Education, 23*(3), 99–113.

Justice, L.M., & Schuele, M. (2004). Phonological awareness: Description, assessment, and intervention. In J. Bernthal & N. Bankson (Eds.), *Articulation and phonological disorders* (5th ed., pp. 376–405). Boston: Allyn & Bacon.

Justice, L.M., Weber, S., Ezell, H.K., & Bakeman, R. (2002). A sequential analysis of children's responsiveness to parental references to print during shared storybook reading. *American Journal of Speech-Language Pathology, 11*, 30–40.

Kaderavek, J.N., & Sulzby, E. (2000). Narrative production by children with and without specific language impairment: Oral narratives and emergent readings. *Journal of Speech, Language, & Hearing Research, 43*(1), 34–49.

Kauffman, J.M. (1999). How we prevent the prevention of emotional and behavioral disorders. *Exceptional Children, 65*(4), 448–468.

Labov, W. (1972). *Language in the inner city: Studies of the black English vernacular*. Philadelphia: University of Pennsylvania Press.

Leseman, P.P.M., & de Jong, P.F. (1998). Home literacy: Opportunity, instruction, cooperation, and social-emotional quality predicting early reading achievement. *Reading Research Quarterly, 33*(3), 294–318.

Lidz, C.S., & Pena, E.D. (1996). Dynamic assessment: The model, its relevance as a nonbiased approach, and its application to Latino American preschool children. *Language, Speech, & Hearing Services in Schools, 27*(4), 367–372.

Lomax, R.G., & McGee, L.M. (1987). Young children's concepts about print and reading: Toward a model of word reading acquisition. *Reading Research Quarterly, 22*(2), 237–256.

Lonigan, C.J., Bloomfield, B.G., Anthony, J.L., Bacon, K.D., Samwel, C.S., & Phillips, B.M. (1999). Relations among emergent literacy skills, behavior problems, and social competence in preschool children from low- and middle-income backgrounds. *Topics in Early Childhood Special Education, 19*(1), 40–53.

Lonigan, C.J., Burgess, S.R., Anthony, J.L., & Barker, T.A. (1998). Development of phonological sensitivity in two- to five-year-old children. *Journal of Educational Psychology, 90*(2), 294–311.

McBride-Chang, C. (1999). The ABCs of the ABCs: The development of letter-name and letter-sound knowledge. *Merrill-Palmer Quarterly, 45*(2), 285–308.

McCabe, A., & Peterson, C. (1984). What makes a good story? *Journal of Psycholinguistic Research, 13,* 457–480.

McGill-Franzen, A., Lanford, C., & Adams, E. (2002). Learning to be literate: A comparison of five urban early childhood programs. *Journal of Educational Psychology, 94*(3), 443–464.

Merritt, D.D., Culatta, B., & Trostle, S. (1998). Narratives: Implementing a discourse framework. In D.D. Merritt & B. Culatta (Eds.), *Language intervention in the classroom* (pp. 277–330). San Diego, CA: Singular.

Nagy, W.E., Anderson, R.C., & Herman, P.A. (1987). Learning word meanings from context during normal reading. *American Educational Research Journal, 24*(2), 237–270.

National Institute of Child Health and Human Development (NICHD). (2000a). *Report of the National Reading Panel. Teaching children to read: An evidence-based assessment of the scientific research literature on reading and its implications for reading instruction* (NIH Publication No. 00-4769). Washington, DC: U.S. Government Printing Office.

National Institute of Child Health and Human Development (NICHD). (2000b). *Report of the National Reading Panel. Teaching children to read: An evidence-based assessment of the scientific research literature on reading and its implications for reading instruction: Reports of the subgroups* (NIH Publication No. 00-4754). Washington, DC: U.S. Government Printing Office.

No Child Left Behind Act of 2001, Public Law 107-110, 34 C.F.R. 200 (January 8, 2002).

Owens, R.E. (2005). *Language development: An introduction* (6th ed.). Boston: Pearson/Allyn & Bacon.

Pence, K.L. (2004). *The input surrounding action verbs in speech to infants and toddlers.* Unpublished doctoral dissertation, University of Delaware.

Penno, J.F., Wilkinson, I.A.G., & Moore, D.W. (2002). Vocabulary acquisition from teacher explanation and repeated listening to stories: Do they overcome the Matthew effect? *Journal of Educational Psychology, 94*(1), 23–33.

Peterson, C. (1990). The who, when, and where of early narratives. *Journal of Child Language, 17*(2), 433–455.

Peterson, C., Jesso, B., & McCabe, A. (1999). Encouraging narratives in preschoolers: An intervention study. *Journal of Child Language, 26*(1), 49–67.

Phillips, G., & McNaughton, S. (1990). The practice of storybook reading to preschool children in mainstream New Zealand families. *Reading Research Quarterly, 25*(3), 196–212.

Pianta, R.C. (1999). *Enhancing relationships between children and teachers.* Washington, DC: American Psychological Association.

Pianta, R.C., & La Paro, K. (2003). Improving early school success. *Educational Leadership, 60*(7), 24–29.

Pianta, R.C., Nimetz, S.L., & Bennett, E. (1997). Mother-child relationships, teacher-child relationships, and school outcomes in preschool and kindergarten. *Early Childhood Research Quarterly, 12,* 263–280.

Pinker, S. (1994). *The language instinct.* New York: William Morrow.

Rathbun, A., & West, J. (2004). *From kindergarten through third grade: Children's beginning school experiences.* (NCES Publication No. 2004007). U.S. Department of Education, National Center for Education Statistics. Washington, DC: U.S. Government Printing Office. Retrieved October 10, 2004, from http://nces.ed.gov/pubsearch/pubsinfo.asp?pubid=2004007

Rimm-Kaufman, S.E., Pianta, R.C., & Cox, M.J. (2000). Teachers' judgments of problems in the transition to kindergarten. *Early Childhood Research Quarterly, 15*(2), 147–166.

Robbins, C., & Ehri, L.C. (1994). Reading storybooks to kindergartners helps them learn new vocabulary words. *Journal of Educational Psychology, 86*(1), 54–64.

Robinson, C., Larsen, J., Haupt, J., & Mohlman, J. (1997). Picture book selection behaviors of emergent readers: Influence of genre, familiarity and book attributes. *Reading Research & Instruction, 36*(4), 287–304.

Sameroff, A.J. (1989). Principles of development and psychopathology. In A.J. Sameroff & R.N. Emde (Eds.), *Relationship disturbances in early childhood: A developmental approach* (pp. 17–32). New York: Basic Books.

Schatschneider, C., Francis, D.J., Foorman, B.R., Fletcher, J.M., & Mehta, P. (1999). The dimensionality of phonological awareness: An application of item response theory. *Journal of Educational Psychology, 91*, 439–449.

Schneider, P., & Hecht, B.F. (1995). Interaction between children with developmental delays and their mothers during a book-sharing activity. *International Journal of Disability, Development, and Education, 42*(1), 41–56.

Senechal, M. (1997). The differential effect of storybook reading on preschoolers' acquisition of expressive and receptive vocabulary. *Journal of Child Language, 24*(1), 123–138.

Senechal, M., LeFevre, L., Thomas, E.M., & Daley, K.E. (1998). Differential effects of home literacy experiences on the development of oral and written language. *Reading Research Quarterly, 33*(1), 96–116.

Senechal, M., Thomas, E.M., & Monker, J. (1995). Individual differences in 4-year-old children's acquisition of vocabulary during storybook reading. *Journal of Educational Psychology, 87*, 218–229.

Skibbe, L., Behnke, M., & Justice, L. (in press). Parental scaffolding of children's phonological awareness skills: Interactions between mothers and their preschoolers with language difficulties. *Communication Disorders Quarterly.*

Smolkin, L., & Donovan, C.A. (2003). Supporting comprehension acquisition for emerging and struggling readers: The interactive information book read-aloud. *Exceptionality, 11*(1), 25–38.

Snow, C.E., Burns, M.S., & Griffin, P. (Eds.). (1998). *Preventing reading difficulties in young children.* Washington, DC: National Academy Press.

Sonnenschein, S., & Munsterman, K. (2002). The influence of home-based reading interactions on 5-year-olds' reading motivations and early literacy development. *Early Childhood Research Quarterly, 17*, 317–338.

Sorsby, A.J., & Martlew, M. (1991). Representational demands in mothers' talk to preschool children in two contexts: Picture book reading and a modeling task. *Journal of Child Language, 18*(2), 373–395.

Stahl, S.A., & Murray, B.A. (1994). Defining phonological awareness and its relationship to early reading. *Journal of Educational Psychology, 86*(2), 221–234.

Stanovich, K.E. (2000). *Progress in understanding reading.* New York: Guilford Press.

Stanovich, P.J., & Stanovich, K.E. (2003). *Using research and reason in education: How teachers can use scientifically based research to make curricular and instructional decisions.* Washington, DC: Partnership for Reading Project, National Institute for Literacy.

Storch, S.A., & Whitehurst, G.J. (2002). Oral language and code-related precursors to reading: Evidence from a longitudinal structural model. *Developmental Psychology, 38*(6), 934–947.

Stothard, S.E., Snowling, M.J., Bishop, D.V.M., Chipchase, B.B., & Kaplan, C.A. (1998). Language impaired preschoolers: A follow-up into adolescence. *Journal of Speech, Language, & Hearing Research, 41*(2), 407–418.

Stuart, M. (1995). Prediction and qualitative assessment of five- and six-year old children's reading: A longitudinal study. *British Journal of Educational Psychology, 65*(3), 287–296.

Teale, W.H. (1986). Home background and young children's literacy development. In W.H. Teale & E. Sulzby (Eds.), *Emergent literacy: Writing and reading* (pp. 173–206). Norwood, NJ: Ablex.

Torgesen, J.K. (1998). Catch them before they fall: Identification and assessment to prevent reading failure in young children. *American Educator, 22*(1–2), 32–39.

Torgesen, J.K., Wagner, R., & Rashotte, C. (1994). Longitudinal studies of phonological processing and reading. *Journal of Learning Disabilities, 27*(5), 276–286.

Treiman, R., & Broderick, V. (1998). What's in a name: Children's knowledge about the letters in their own names. *Journal of Experimental Child Psychology, 70*(2), 97–116.

Ukrainetz, T.A. (1998). Beyond Vygotsky: What Soviet activity theory offers naturalistic language intervention. *Journal of Speech-Language Pathology & Audiology, 22*, 122–133.

van Kleeck, A. (1998). Preliteracy domains and stages: Laying the foundations for beginning reading. *Journal of Children's Communication Development, 20*(1), 33–51.

van Kleeck, A., Stahl, S.A., & Bauer, E.B. (Eds.). (2003). *On reading books to children: Parents and teachers.* Mahwah, NJ: Erlbaum.

Vukelich, C. (1994). Effects of play interventions on young children's reading of environmental print. *Early Childhood Research Quarterly, 9*(2), 153–170.

Vygotsky, L. (1978). *Mind in society* (A. Cole, V. John-Steiner, S. Scribner, & E. Souberman, Eds. & Trans.). Cambridge, MA: Harvard University Press. (Original work published 1930)

Vygotsky, L. (1986). *Thought and language* (A. Kozulin, Ed. & Trans.). Cambridge, MA: MIT Press. (Original work published 1934)

Walpole, S., Chow, S.M., & Justice, L.M. (2004). Literacy achievements during kindergarten: Examining key contributors in an at-risk sample. *Early Education & Development, 15*(3), 245–264.

Wasik, B.A., & Bond, M.A. (2001). Beyond the pages of a book: Interactive book reading and language development in preschool classrooms. *Journal of Educational Psychology, 93*(2), 243–250.

Watkins, R.V., & Bunce, B.H. (1996). Natural literacy: Theory and practice for preschool intervention programs. *Topics in Early Childhood Special Education, 16*(2), 191–212.

Weitzman, E., & Greenberg, J. (2002). *Learning language and loving it: A guide to promoting children's social and language development in early childhood settings* (2nd ed.). Toronto, ON, Canada: Hanen Centre.

Welsch, J.G., Sullivan, A.K., & Justice, L.M. (2003). That's my letter! What preschoolers' name writing representations can tell us about emergent literacy knowledge. *Journal of Literacy Research, 35*, 757–776.

Whitehurst, G.J., Arnold, D.H., Epstein, J.N., Angell, A.L., Smith, M., & Fiscehl, J.E. (1994). A picture book reading intervention in day care and home for children from low-income families. *Developmental Psychology, 30*(5), 679–689.

Whitehurst, G.J., & Lonigan, C.J. (1998). Child development and emergent literacy. *Child Development, 69*(3), 848–872.

Woodward, A.L. (1999). Infants' ability to distinguish between purposeful and non-purposeful behaviors. *Infant Behavior and Development, 22*, 145–160.

Woodward, A.L., Sommerville, J.A., & Guajardo, J.J. (2001). How infants make sense of intentional action. In B.F. Malle, L.J. Moses, & D.A. Baldwin (Eds.), *Intentions and intentionality: Foundations of social cognition* (pp. 149–169). Cambridge, MA: MIT Press.

Yaden, D.B., Jr., Smolkin, L.B., & Conlon, A. (1989). Preschoolers' questions about pictures, print conventions and story text during reading aloud at home. *Reading Research Quarterly, 24*(2), 188–214.

CHILDREN'S LITERATURE CITED

Aardema, V. (1981). *Bringing the rain to Kapiti Plain* (B. Vidal, Illus.). New York: Dial Press.

Abercrombie, B. (1990). *Charlie Anderson* (M. Graham, Illus.). New York: M.K. McElderry Books.

Alborough, J. (2000). *Hug*. Cambridge, MA: Candlewick Press.

Andreae, G. (1997). *Rumble in the jungle* (D. Wojtowycz, Illus.). Wilton, CT: Tiger Tales.

Amery, H. (2003). *Where's Curly?* (S. Cartwright, Illus.). Tulsa, OK: E.D.C. Publishing.

Appelt, K. (1993). *Elephants aloft* (K. Baker, Illus.). San Diego, CA: Harcourt Brace Jovanovich.

Barrett, J. (1978). *Cloudy with a chance of meatballs* (R. Barrett, Illus.). New York: Atheneum.

Barton, B. (2001). *My car*. New York: Greenwillow Books.

Beaton, C. (2000). *How big is a pig?* (S. Blackstone, Illus.). Cambridge, MA: Barefoot Books.

Berenstain, S., & Berenstain, J. (1988). *The Berenstain Bears ready, get set, go!* New York: Random House.

Bridwell, N. (1988). *Clifford's birthday party*. New York: Scholastic.

Brown, M.W. (1942). *The runaway bunny* (C. Hurd, Illus.). New York: HarperCollins.

Burningham, J. (1970). *Mr. Gumpy's outing*. New York: Holt, Rinehart & Winston.

Campbell, R. (1982). *Dear zoo*. New York: Four Winds Press.

Carle, E. (1984). *The very busy spider*. New York: Philomel.

Carle, E. (1994). *The very hungry caterpillar*. New York: Philomel.

Charles, D. (1981). *Calico cat at the zoo*. Chicago: Children's Press.

Cousins, L. (2001). *Maisy at the fair*. Cambridge, MA: Candlewick Press.

Cowen-Fletcher, J. (1993). *Mama zooms*. New York: Scholastic.

Cox, P.R. (2000). *Sam Sheep can't sleep* (S. Cartwright, Illus.). London: Usborne Books.

Cox, P.R. (2001). *Goose on the loose* (S. Cartwright, Illus.). Tulsa, OK: E.D.C. Publishing.

Crews, D. (1978). *Freight train*. New York: Greenwillow.

Crews, D. (1982). *Harbor*. New York: Greenwillow.

Crews, D. (1984). *School bus*. New York: Greenwillow.

Crews, D. (1986). *Flying*. New York: Greenwillow.

Crews, D. (1995). *Sail away*. New York: Greenwillow.

Cronin, D. (2003). *Diary of a worm* (H. Bliss, Illus.). New York: Joanna Cotler.

Drew, D. (1994). *Nibbly Mouse* (P. Newman, Illus.). Santa Rosa, CA: SRA School Group.

DuQuette, K. (2002). *They call me Woolly: What animal names can tell us*. New York: Putnam.

Egielski, R. (1997). *The Gingerbread Boy*. New York: Laura Geringer Books.

Ehlert, L. (1987). *Growing vegetable soup*. San Diego: Harcourt Brace Jovanovich.

Ehlert, L. (1991). *Red leaf, yellow leaf*. San Diego: Harcourt Brace Jovanovich.

Ehlert, L. (1998). *Top cat*. San Diego: Harcourt Brace.

Fleming, D. (1991). *In the tall, tall grass*. New York: Henry Holt.

Fleming, D. (1992). *Count!* New York: Henry Holt.

Fleming, D. (1993). *In the small, small pond*. New York: Henry Holt.

Fleming, D. (1998). *Mama cat has three kittens*. New York: Henry Holt.

Florian, D. (1994). *Beast feast*. San Diego: Harcourt Brace.

Freeman, D. (1968). *Corduroy*. New York: Viking Press.

Freymann, S., & Elffers, J. (1999). *How are you peeling? Foods with moods*. New York: Arthur A. Levine Books.

Hall, Z. (2000). *Fall leaves fall!* (S. Halpern, Illus.). New York: Scholastic.

Hausman, B. (1999). *A to Z, do you ever feel like me? A guessing alphabet of feelings, words, and other cool stuff* (S. Fellman, Photog.). New York: Dutton's Children's Books.

Hawkins, C., & Hawkins, J. (1995). *Zug the bug*. London: Piccadilly Press.

Hazen, B.S. (1970). *Where do bears sleep?* (I.E. Staunton, Illus.). Reading, MA: Addison-Wesley.

Hill, E. (1981). *Spot's first walk.* New York: Putnam.

Hill, E. (1987). *Spot goes to the farm.* New York: Putnam.

Hoban, T. (1983). *I read signs.* New York: Greenwillow Books.

Hoban, T. (1987). *26 letters and 99 cents.* New York: Greenwillow Books.

Hoban, T. (1990). *Exactly the opposite.* New York: Greenwillow Books.

Jonas, A. (1997). *Watch William walk.* New York: Greenwillow Books.

Jones, C. (Illus.). (2000). *This old man.* Boston: Houghton Mifflin.

Keats, E.J. (1962). *The snowy day.* London: Bodley Head.

Kellogg, S. (2001). *A penguin pup for Pinkerton.* New York: Dial Books for Young Readers.

Kroll, V. (2003). *Busy, busy mouse* (F. Kosaka, Illus.). New York: Viking.

Leedy, L. (2000). *Mapping Penny's world.* New York: Henry Holt.

Lewis, K., & Kirk, D. (2002). *My truck is stuck!* New York: Hyperion Books for Children.

Lindbergh, R. (1997). *The awful aardvarks go to school* (T.C. Pearson, Illus.). New York: Viking.

Lionni, L. (1970). *Fish is fish.* New York: Pantheon Books.

Lionni, L. (1973). *Swimmy.* New York: Random House.

Lobel, A. (1994). *Away from home.* New York: Greenwillow.

London, J. (1992). *Froggy gets dressed* (F. Remkiewicz, Illus.). New York: Viking.

London, J. (1999). *Froggy plays soccer* (F. Remkiewicz, Illus.). New York: Viking.

Martin, B., Jr. (1992). *Brown bear, brown bear, what do you see?* (E. Carle, Illus.). New York: Henry Holt. (Original work published 1967)

Martin, B., Jr, & Archambault, J. (1989). *Chicka chicka boom boom* (L. Ehlert, Illus.). New York: Simon & Schuster Books for Young Readers.

Maslen, B.L. (1999). *The big hat.* New York: Scholastic.

McMillan, B. (1989). *Super, super, superwords.* New York: Lothrop, Lee & Shepard.

Merriam, E. (1993). *12 ways to get to 11* (B. Karlin, Illus.). New York: Simon & Schuster Books for Young Readers.

Morris, A. (1998). *Tools* (K. Heyman, Illus.). New York: Mulberry.

Moss, L. (1995). *Zin! Zin! Zin! A violin* (M. Priceman, Illus.). New York: Simon & Schuster Books for Young Readers.

Noll, S. (1987). *Jiggle, wiggle, prance.* New York: Greenwillow Books.

Numeroff, L.J. (1985). *If you give a mouse a cookie* (F. Bond, Illus.). New York: Harper & Row.

Numeroff, L.J. (1991). *If you give a moose a muffin* (F. Bond, Illus.). New York: HarperCollins.

Numeroff, L.J. (1998). *If you give a pig a pancake* (F. Bond, Illus.). New York: Laura Geringer.

Peck, J. (1998). *The giant carrot.* New York: Dial Books for Young Readers.

Penn, A. (1993). *The kissing hand* (R.E. Harper & N.M. Leak, Illus.). Washington, DC: Child Welfare League of America.

Priddy, R. (1996). *My big book of everything.* New York: DK Publishing.

Rathmann, P. (1994). *Good night, Gorilla.* New York: Putnam.

Rathmann, P. (1998). *10 minutes till bedtime.* New York: G.P. Putnam's Sons.

Rosen, M. (1992). *We're going on a bear hunt* (H. Oxenbury, Illus.). New York: Aladdin Books.

Seuss, Dr. (2002). *The foot book.* New York: Random House. (Original work published 1968)

Shannon, D. (2000). *The rain came down.* New York: Blue Sky Press.

Shannon, D. (2002). *David gets in trouble.* New York: Blue Sky Press.

Shaw, N. (1986). *Sheep in a jeep* (M. Apple, Illus.). Boston: Houghton Mifflin.

Shaw, N. (1991). *Sheep in a shop* (M. Apple, Illus.). Boston: Houghton Mifflin.

Shaw, N. (1992). *Sheep out to eat* (M. Apple, Illus.). Boston: Houghton Mifflin.

Silverstein, S. (1976). *The missing piece.* New York: Harper & Row.

Simmons, J. (1998). *Come along, Daisy!* Boston: Little, Brown.

Sis, P. (1999). *Trucks, trucks, trucks.* New York: Greenwillow Books.

Steig, W. (1998). *Pete's a pizza*. New York: HarperCollins.

Taback, S. (1997). *There was an old lady who swallowed a fly*. New York: Viking.

Teague, M. (2002). *Dear Mrs. LaRue: Letters from obedience school*. New York: Scholastic.

Treays, R. (1998). *My street* (R. Wells, Illus.). Tulsa, OK: E.D.C. Publishing.

Vail, R. (2002). *Sometimes I'm Bombaloo* (Y. Heo, Illus.). New York: Scholastic.

Willems, M. (2003). *Don't let the pigeon drive the bus*. New York: Hyperion Books for Children.

Williams, S. (1990). *I went walking* (J. Vivas, Illus.). San Diego, CA: Harcourt Brace Jovanovich.

Wilson, K. (2001). *Bear snores on* (J. Chapman, Illus.). New York: Margaret K. McElderry Books.

INDEX

A

A to Z, Do You Ever Feel Like Me? (Hausman, B.), 32–33

Aardema, V., 94

Abercrombie, B., 93

accountability, viii

action verbs, 31–32, 75

action–result sequences, 31, 32

activities: for alphabet knowledge, 56–66; for narrative knowledge, 72–80; for phonological awareness, 43–50; for print knowledge, 16–22; for word knowledge, 29–37, 87–89; for world knowledge, 86–92

Adams, E., 1

Adams, M.J., xii, 14

adjectives, 34–35, 38, 39

adult scaffolding. *See* scaffolding

adult–child storybook interactions. *See* interactive book reading

adverbs, 73–74, 75

Alborough, J., 67

alliteration, 41

The Alphabet Cat activity, 62–64

alphabet knowledge: activities addressing, 56–66; benefits of, xii; and culture, 54; definition of, 7; development of, 53–55; importance of, 6; interactive book reading to support, 56–66; overview of, 53; storybooks for building, 66–68; tips for parents regarding, 55

alphabetic code, 6

An Alphabetic Tour activity, 91–92

Amery, H., 51

Anderson, R.C., 27

Andreae, G., 67

Angell, A.L., ix, 76

animals, 92–93

Anthony, J.L., xii, 2, 6

Appelt, K., 38

Archambault, J., 50

Arnold, D.H., ix, 76

at-risk students, 2–3

Attention to Action activity, 29–31

Awareness of Characters activity, 74–76

Away From Home (Lobel, A.), 91–92

The Awful Aardvarks Go to School (Lindbergh, R.), 58–60

B

Bacon, K.D., 2

Bailey, D., 42

Bakeman, R., 64

Baker, L., 54

Barker, T.A., 6

Barrett, J., 80

Barton, B., 23

Bauer, E.B., 1

Bear, D.R., 43

Bear Snores On (Wilson, K.), 50

Beast Feast (Florian, D.), 89–90

Beaton, C., 35–37

Beck, I.L., xi

Beckman, A., x, xi

beginning sounds, 48–49, 50, 91

Behnke, M., 43

Bennett, E., 84

The Berenstain Bears Ready, Set, Go! (Berenstain, S., & Berenstain, J.), 37–38

Berenstain, J., 37–38

Berenstain, S., 37–38

Berko Gleason, J., 4

The Big Hat (Maslen, B.L.), 49–50

Bishop, D.V.M., 41

Bloomfield, B.G., 2

Bond, M.A., ix, 12

Bowey, J.A., 2, 54

Brent, M.R., 26

Bridwell, N., 78–80

Bringing the Rain to Kapiti Plain (Aardema, V.), 94

Brinton, B., 3

Broderick, V., 54

Brown Bear, Brown Bear, What Do You See? (Martin, B., Jr), 21–22

Brown, M.W., 81

Brown, R., 36

Bruner, J.S., 9

Bryant, P.E., 41

Bunce, B.H., 42

BURGESS, S.R., xii, 6
BURNINGHAM, J., 29–31
BURNS, M.S., 3, 14, 15, 27, 28
BURNS, T.C., 34
BUS, A.G., 8, 11
BUSY, BUSY MOUSE (KROLL, V.), 43–45

C

CALICO CAT AT THE ZOO (CHARLES, D.), 38
CAMPBELL, R., 66
CARLE, E., 31–32, 73–74
CARROLL, J.M., 41
CATTS, H.W., 3
CHALL, J.S., 5
CHANEY, C., 2, 6, 54
CHARACTER, 93
CHARLES, D., 38
CHARLIE ANDERSON (ABERCROMBIE, B.), 93
CHICKA CHICKA BOOM BOOM (MARTIN, B., JR, &
    ARCHAMBAULT, J.), 50
CHILDREN, RISK FACTORS OF, viii, 2–3
CHIPCHASE, B.B., 41
CHOI, S., 34
CHOW, S.M., 53, 55
CLARKE, D., 3
CLIFFORD'S BIRTHDAY PARTY (BRIDWELL, N.), 78–80
CLOUDY WITH A CHANCE OF MEATBALLS (BARRETT, J.), 80
COME ALONG, DAISY! (SIMMONS, J.), 22
COMMENTS: in alphabet knowledge activities,
    57–58; vs. questions, ix
COMPARISONS, 39
COMPOUND WORDS, 45–46
COMPREHENSION, 28–29
CONLON, A., 1, 13
CORDUROY (FREEMAN, D.), 80
COUNT! (FLEMING, D.), 94
COUSINS, L., 67
COWEN-FLETCHER, J., 93
COX, M.J., viii, 3
COX, P.R., 51
CRAIN-THORESON, C., ix
CREWS, D., 57–58, 66–67
CRONIN, D., 76–77
CULATTA, B., 70
CULTURE: and alphabet knowledge, 54; and
    interactive book reading, 1; storybooks
    involving, 94–95

D

DALE, P.S., ix
DALEY, K.E., 53
DAVID GETS IN TROUBLE (SHANNON, D.), 66
DE JONG, P.F., 11
DEAR MRS. LARUE: LETTERS FROM OBEDIENCE SCHOOL
    (TEAGUE, M.), 66
DEAR ZOO (CAMPBELL, R.), 66
DECONTEXTUALIZED MONOLOGUES, 69
DIARY OF A WORM (CRONIN, D.), 76–77
DIAZ, R.M., 9, 10
DICKINSON, D.K., 1
DISTANCING SCAFFOLDS, 9
DONOVAN, C.A., 86
DON'T LET THE PIGEON DRIVE THE BUS (WILLEMS, M.),
    22–23
DREW, D., 64–66
DRISCOLL, K., xii
DUQUETTE, K., 34–35

E

ECONOMICALLY DISADVANTAGED CHILDREN, 2–3
EDUCATORS: relationship of children with, 84; role
    of, 56
EGIELSKI, R., 80
EGOCENTRIC THINKING, 62
EHLERT, L., 18–20, 62–64, 87–88, 92
EHRI, L.C., xi, 5, 12, 27
ELEPHANTS ALOFT (APPELT, K.), 38
ELFFERS, J., 38
ELLEY, W.B., 27
EMOTIONS, 32–33, 38, 39
ENDING ON A SAME NOTE ACTIVITY, 49–50
ENGAGEMENT, 11–12
ENHANCING LANGUAGE WITH DESCRIPTIVE WORDS
    ACTIVITY, 34–35
ENVIRONMENTAL PRINT: activities addressing, 90–91;
    parental tips regarding, 14, 15
EPSTEIN, J.N., ix, 76
EXACTLY THE OPPOSITE (HOBAN, T.), 38
EXTENDING, 43
EZELL, H.K., ix, 2, 6, 10, 13, 14–15, 54, 56, 64

F

FACE-TO-FACE POSITIONING, 11, 28
FALL LEAVES FALL! (HALL, Z.), 23
FEELINGS, 32–33, 38, 39

Fernandez-Fein, S., 54
Feuerstein, R., 10
Fey, M.E., 3
final sounds, 49–50
Fischel, J.E., ix, 76
Fish Is Fish (Lionni, L.), 93
Fleming, D., 20–21, 46–47, 51, 94
Fletcher, J.M., 2, 40
Florian, D., 89–90
focused stimulation, 74
Foorman, B.R., 40
The Foot Book (Seuss, Dr.), 38
Fox, B., 44
Francis, D.J., 2, 40
Freeman, D., 80
Freight Train (Crews, D.), 66–67
Freymann, S., 38
Froggy Gets Dressed (London, J.), 50
Froggy Plays Soccer (London, J.), 67
Fujiki, M., 3

G

Ganger, J., 26
genres, 85–86
Gentner, D., 30
geography, 94–95
The Giant Carrot (Peck, J.), 77–78
The Gingerbread Boy (Egielski, R.), 80
Girolametto, L., 10, 74
Goldfield, B.A., 26
Good Night, Gorilla (Rathmann, P.), 23, 80
Goodman, Y.M., 13
Goose on the Loose (Cox, P.R.), 51
Gopnik, A., 34
Goswami, U., 41
Gough, P.B., 5
Greehalgh, K.S., 77
Greenberg, J., 11, 28
Greenfield, P.M., 10
Griffin, P., 3, 14, 15, 27, 28
Growing Vegetable Soup (Ehlert, L.), 18–20, 92–93
Guajardo, J.J., 31

H

Hall, D.G., 34
Hall, Z., 23
Hammett, L.A., 1
Hart, B., 27
Haryu, E., 30
Haupt, J., 85
Hausman, B., 32–33
Hawkins, C., 81–82
Hawkins, J., 81–82
Hazen, B.S., 93
Head Start program, 56
Hecht, B.F., 11
Hegde, M.N., 70
Herman, P.A., 27
Hiebert, E.H., 14
high point, of story, 78–80
Hill, E., 24, 68
Hoban, T., 38, 68, 90–91
Hoff, E., 4, 27
Hoff-Ginsberg, E., 2
How Are You Peeling? Foods With Moods (Freymann, S., & Elffers, J.), 38
How Big Is a Pig? (Beaton, C.), 35–37
Huberty, C.J., 1
Hug (Alborough, J.), 67
Hulme, C., 41
Hutchison, J.K., 71

I

I Read Signs (Hoban, T.), 90–91
I Went Walking (Williams, S.), 16–17
If I Had a Hammer activity, 88–89
If You Give a Moose a Muffin (Numeroff, L.), 17–18
If You Give a Mouse a Cookie (Numeroff, L.), 23
If You Give a Pig a Pancake (Numeroff, L.), 45–46
illustrations, 13
Imai, M., 30
In the Small, Small, Pond (Fleming, D.), 51
In the Tall, Tall Grass (Fleming, D.), 46–47
informational books, 86
intentionality, 1
interactive book reading: benefits of, viii–ix; characteristics of effective, 10–13; and culture, 1; definition of, 1; description of, 1, 8; role of, 7–10; as structural scaffold, 10; to support alphabet knowledge, 56–66; to support narrative knowledge, 72–80; to support phonological awareness, 42–50; to support print knowledge, 14–22; to support word knowledge, 27–37; to support world knowledge, 85–92; variability in, 1
interactive reading activities. *See* activities
Invernizzi, M., 43

J

Jesso, B., 72
Jiggle, Wiggle, Prance (Noll, S.), 39
Johnson, C., viii
Johnston, F., 43
Jonas, A., 41
Jones, C., 60–62
Juel, C., vii
Justice, L.M., ix–x, 2, 6, 10, 12, 13, 14–15, 27, 41, 43, 53, 54, 55, 56, 64

K

Kaderavek, J.N., 70, 78
Kaplan, C.A., 41
Kauffman, J.M., 3
Keats, E.J., 81
Keebler, R., 1
Kellogg, S., 81
kindergarten educators, vii–viii
Kirk, D., 81
The Kissing Hand (Penn, A.), 94
knowledge bases, vii, 83
Kroll, V., 43–45
Kucan, L., xi

L

La Paro, K., 1, 4
labels, 15
Labov, W., 69, 79
Lanford, C., 1
language: definition of, 4; development of, 4, 5–6; domains of, 4–5; role of interactive reading in, 7–10
Lankford, C., 13
Larsen, J., 85
Leedy, L., 94–95
LeFevre, L., 53
Leseman, P.P.M., 11
Letters on the Bus activity, 57–58
Letters on the Ground activity, 58–60
Lewis, K., 81
Lidz, C.S., 9
life issues, 93–94
Lindbergh, R., 58–60
linguistic scaffolds, 9–10
Lionni, L., 93

listening, 11, 28
literacy: definition of, 5; development of, 4, 5–6; and poverty, 2–3; role of interactive reading in, 7–10
literacy-rich environment, 14
literate language, 72
Lobel, A., 91–92
Location, Location, Location activity, 76–77
Lomax, R.G., 14
London, J., 50, 67
Lonigan, C.J., xii, 2, 6, 8
Look Who's Talking activity, 77–78
lowercase letters, 59, 68

M

Maisy at the Fair (Cousins, L.), 67
Mama Cat Has Three Kittens (Fleming, D.), 20–21
Mama Zooms (Cowen-Fletcher, J.), 93
Mapping Penny's World (Leedy, L.), 94–95
Martin, B., Jr, 22–22, 50
Martlew, M., 28
Maslen, B.L., 49–50
McBride-Chang, C., 54
McCabe, A., 72, 79
McGee, L.M., 14
McGill-Franzen, A., 1
McKeown, M.G., xi
McMillan, B., 39
McNaughton, S., 13
Mehta, P., 40
Meier, J., 27
memorization, 14
mental concepts, 32–33
Merriam, E., 94
Merritt, D.D., 70
The Missing Piece (Silverstein, S.), 93
modeling, 43
Mohlman, J., 85
money, 94
Monker, J., xi
Moore, D.W., ix, 12, 27
morphology: definition of, 4; development of, 5; of verbs, 30
Morris, A., 88–89
Moss, L., 51–52
Mr. Grumpy's Outing (Burningham, J.), 29–31
Munsterman, K., 1
Murray, B.A., 40
My Big Book of Everything (Priddy, R.), 95

My Car (Barton, B.), 23
My Street (Treays, R.), 23–24
My Truck Is Stuck! (Lewis, K., & Kirk, D.), 81

N

Nagy, W.E., 27
Naigles, L., 27
names, 62
narrative knowledge: activities addressing,
    72–80; definition of, xii, 68; development of,
    69–71; interactive book reading to support,
    72–80; overview of, 69; storybooks for
    building, 80–82; tips for parents regarding,
    71
National Institute of Child Health and Human
    Development (NICHD), 6, 26, 27, 29
nature books, 92–93
Neal, C., 9, 10
Nibbly Mouse (Drew, D.), 64–66
NICHD. *See* National Institute of Child Health
    and Human Development
Nimetz, S.L., 84
No Child Left Behind Act (2001), 2
Noll, S., 39
nonfiction books, 86
nonverbal references, 19, 21
numbers, 94
Numeroff, L., 17–18, 23, 45–46

O

observing, 11
Okada, H., 30
The Old Man's Alphabet activity, 60–62
On the Contrary activity, 35–37
onsets, 41
open-ended questions, 28, 76
opposites, 35–37, 38
oral language register, 78
Owens, R.E., 4
own-name advantage, 54

P–Q

parents: alphabet knowledge tips for, 55;
    narrative knowledge tips for, 71;
    phonological awareness tips for, 42; print
    knowledge tips for, 15; word knowledge tips
    for, 28; world knowledge tips for, 85

Pawluski, J.L., 34
Pearce, P.S., 10, 74
Peck, J., 77–78
Pena, E.D., 9
Pence, K.L., x
A Penguin Pup for Pinkerton (Kellogg, S.), 81
Penn, A., 94
Penno, J.F., ix, 12, 27
persistence, 11–12
Peterson, C., 70, 72, 79
Pete's a Pizza (Steig, W.), 74–76
Phillips, B.M., xii, 2
Phillips, G., 13
phonics, 55
phonological awareness: activities addressing,
    43–50; benefits of, xi–xii; definition of, xi, 7;
    development of, 7, 40–41; importance of, 6;
    interactive book reading to support, 42–50;
    overview of, 40; storybooks for building,
    50–52; tips for parents regarding, 42
phonology, 4, 5
Pianta, R.C., viii, 1, 3, 4, 84
Pinker, S., 26
plant life cycle, 87–88
poetry, 86, 90
poverty, 2–3
pragmatics, 5
prepositions, 35–37, 38
Preschool Language and Literacy Lab (University
    of Virginia), ix
Priddy, R., 95
primary prevention, 3
print conventions, 6, 14
print forms, 6
print functions, 6, 14
print interest, 6
print knowledge: activities addressing, 16–22;
    definition of, 7, 13; development of, 13–14;
    interactive book reading to support, 14–22;
    storybooks for building, 22–25; tips for
    parents regarding, 15
print part-to-whole relationships, 6–7
print-referencing strategies, 19, 21
print-related vocabulary, 16–17
props, 88–89
Pullen, P.C., 43
questions: vs. comments, ix; tips for parents
    regarding, 28. *See also specific types*

R

THE RAIN CAME DOWN (SHANNON, D.), 93
RASHOTTE, C., 41
RATHBUN, A., viii
RATHMANN, P., 23, 80, 94
READINESS, 3–4
READING, CHILDREN'S DEVELOPMENT IN, 5–6
READING ACHIEVEMENT, viii
RED LEAF, YELLOW LEAF (EHLERT, L.), 87–88
REGULATORY SCAFFOLDS, 10
RELATIONSHIPS, 84
REPEATED READING, 12
REPETITION, 16, 21–22
REPORTED SPEECH, 77–78
RESPONSIVENESS, 11
REZNICK, J.S., 26
RHYME AWARENESS, 46–47, 51–52
RHYME PRODUCTION, 46–47, 50
RIMES, 41
RIMM-KAUFMAN, S.E., viii, 3
RISK FACTORS, viii, 2–3
RISLEY, T.R., 27
ROBBINS, C., xi, 12, 27
ROBINSON, C., 85
ROSEN, M., 24, 81
ROUTH, D.K., 44
RUMBLE IN THE JUNGLE (ANDREAE, G.), 67
THE RUNAWAY BUNNY (BROWN, M.W.), 81

S

SAM SHEEP CAN'T SLEEP (COX, P.R.), 51
SAMEROFF, A.J., 84
SAMWEL, C.S., 2
SCAFFOLDING: criteria for, 9; definition of, x, 8;
    description of, 8; vs. shaping, 8–9; types of,
    9–10
SCHATSCHNEIDER, C., 40
SCHNEIDER, P., 11
SCHOOL BUS (CREWS, D.), 57–58
SCHOOL READINESS. *See* readiness
SCHUELE, M., 41
SECONDARY PREVENTION, 3
SEGMENTING SENTENCES, 43–46
SEMANTICS, 4, 5
SENECHAL, M., xi, 12, 53
SENSITIVITY, 11
SENTENCE SEGEMENTATION, 43–46
SEQUENCE OF EVENTS, 73–74

SEQUENCING WITH ADVERBS ACTIVITY, 73–74
SETTING, 76–77
SEUSS, DR., 38
SHANNON, D., 66, 93
SHAPING, 8–9
SHARED BOOK READING. *See* interactive book reading
SHAW, N., 24, 48–49, 51
SHAYWITZ, S.E., 2
SHEEP IN A JEEP (SHAW, N.), 24
SHEEP IN A SHOP (SHAW, N.), 48–49
SHEEP OUT TO EAT (SHAW, N.), 51
SHOW ME THE WORDS ACTIVITY, 20–21
SIGNS, SIGNS, EVERYWHERE A SIGN ACTIVITY, 90–91
SILVERSTEIN, S., 93
SIMMONS, J., 22
SIS, P., 39
SKIBBE, L., x, xi, 43
SMITH, M., ix, 76
SMOLKIN, L.B., 1, 13, 86
SNOW, C.E., 3, 14, 15, 27, 28
SNOWLING, M.J., 41
THE SNOWY DAY (KEATS, E.J.), 81
SOMETIMES I'M BOMBALOO (VAIL, R.), 39
SOMMERVILLE, J.A., 31
SONNENSCHEIN, S., 1
SORSBY, A.J., 28
SPOT GOES TO THE FARM (HILL, E.), 24
SPOT'S FIRST WALK (HILL, E.), 68
STAHL, S.A., 1, 40
STANOVICH, K.E., vii, viii
STANOVICH, P.J., viii
START AT THE BEGINNING ACTIVITY, 47–49
STEIG, W., 74–76
STEVENSON, J., 41
STORCH, S.A., xii, 6, 53
THE STORY IS IN THE WORDS ACTIVITY, 18–20
STORYBOOK READING INTERACTIONS. *See* interactive
    book reading
STOTHARD, S.E., 41
STRONG, C.J., 77
STRUCTURAL SCAFFOLDS, 10
STUART, M., 6
STUEBING, K.K., 2
SULLLIVAN, A.K., 54
SULZBY, E., 70, 78
SUPER, SUPER, SUPERWORDS (MCMILLAN, B.), 39
SWIMMY (LIONNI, L.), 93
SYLLABLES, 45–46
SYMBOLS, 90–91
SYNTAX, 4, 5

T

TABACK, S., 51
TAKING APART SENTENCES activity, 43–45
TALKING ABOUT FEELINGS activity, 32–33
TEAGUE, M., 66
TEALE, W.H., 8
TELEPHONE CONVERSATIONS, 71
TEMPLETON, S., 43
10 MINUTES TILL BEDTIME (RATHMANN, P.), 94
TERTIARY PREVENTION, 3
TEXT BUBBLES, 77
TEXT DIRECTIONALITY, 20–21
THERE WAS AN OLD LADY WHO SWALLOWED A FLY
    (TABACK, S.), 51
THEY CALL ME WOOLLY: WHAT ANIMAL NAMES CAN TELL
    US (DUQUETTE, K.), 34–35
THIS OLD MAN (JONES, C.), 60–62
THOMAS, E.M., xi, 53
TIME, 94
TOMBLIN, J.B., 3
TOOLS (MORRIS, A.), 88–89
TOP CAT (EHLERT, L.), 62–64
TORGESEN, J.K., 2, 41
TOYS, 15
TREAYS, R., 23–24
A TREE OF KNOWLEDGE activity, 87–88
TREIMAN, R., 54
TROSTLE, S., 70
TRUCKS, TRUCKS, TRUCKS (SIS, P.), 39
TUNMER, W.E., 5
12 WAYS TO GET TO 11 (MERRIAM, E.), 94
26 LETTERS AND 99 CENTS (HOBAN, T.), 68

U

UKRAINETZ, T.A., 9, 10
UPPERCASE LETTERS, 59, 68
U.S. DEPARTMENT OF EDUCATION, viii

V

VACHIO, A., 9, 10
VAIL, R., 39
VALUES, 93
VAN IJZENDOORN, M.H., 11
VAN KLEECK, A., 1, 13
VERBAL REFERENCES, 19, 21
VERBS: activities regarding, 29–32, 75;
    morphology of, 30

THE VERY BUSY SPIDER (CARLE, E.), 31–32
THE VERY HUNGRY CATERPILLAR (CARLE, E.), 73–74
VOCABULARY. See word knowledge
VUKELICH, C., 91
VYGOTSKY, L., 1, 9

W

WAGNER, R., 41
WAITING, 11, 28
WALPOLE, S., 27, 53, 55
WASIK, B.A., ix, 12
WATCH WILLIAM WALK (JONAS, A.), 41
WATKINS, R.V., 42
WEBER, S., 64
WEITZMAN, E., 10, 11, 28, 74
WELSCH, J.G., 54
WE'RE GOING ON A BEAR HUNT (ROSEN, M.), 24, 81
WEST, J., viii
A WHALE OF A TALE activity, 89–90
WHAT RHYMES WITH THAT? activity, 46–47
WHAT'S IN A WORD? activity, 45–46
WHERE DO BEARS SLEEP? (HAZEN, B.S.), 93
WHERE THE EXCITEMENT IS activity, 78–80
WHERE'S CURLY? (AMERY, H.), 51
WHITEHURST, G.J., xii, ix, 6, 8, 53, 76
WHY WE DO THE THINGS WE DO activity, 31–32
WIGGINS, A., x, xii
WILKINSON, I.A.G., ix, 12, 27
WILLEMS, M., 22–23
WILLIAMS, S., 16–17
WILSON, K., 50
WITHDRAWING SUPPORT, 43
WOODWARD, A.L., 31
WORD AWARENESS, 21–22
WORD KNOWLEDGE: activities addressing, 29–37,
    87–89; and comprehension, 28–29;
    development of, 26–27; and feelings, 33;
    importance of, xi; and informational books,
    86; interactive book reading to support,
    27–37; overview of, 26; and repeated
    reading, 12; storybooks for building, 37–39;
    tips for parents regarding, 28
WORD SEARCH activity, 21–22
WORDS ABOUT PRINT activity, 16–17
WORDS FROM START TO FINISH activity, 17–18
WORLD KNOWLEDGE: activities addressing, 86–92;
    books as source of, xii; development of,
    83–84; interactive reading to support,

85–92; overview of, 83; storybooks for building, 92–95; tips for parents regarding, 85

WRITTEN LANGUAGE AWARENESS, 6

WRITTEN LANGUAGE REGISTER, 78

Y

YADEN, D.B., JR., 1, 13

YES/NO QUESTIONS, 28

Z

ZHANG, X., 3

ZIN! ZIN! ZIN! A VIOLIN (MOSS, L.), 51–52

ZUG THE BUG (HAWKINS, C., & HAWKINS, J.), 81